FLEXI-SCHOOLING

Education for tomorrow, starting yesterday

ROLAND MEIGHAN

EDUCATION NOW BOOKS

Published 1988 by Education Now Publishing Cooperative Limited
P.O.Box 186, Ticknall, Derbyshire DE7 1WF

© Roland Meighan 1988
ISBN 1 871526 00 0

British Library Cataloguing in Publication Data
Meighan, Roland
 Flexi-schooling : education for tomorrow, starting yesterday.
 1. Great Britain. Education. Innovation
 I. Title
 370.941

ISBN 1-871526-00-0

This book is sold subject to the condition that it shall not, by way of trade or otherwise, be lent, re-sold, hired out, or otherwise circulated without the publisher's prior consent in any form of binding or cover other than that in which it is published and without a similar condition including this condition being imposed on the subsequent purchaser

Design Ron Biggs

Printed in Great Britain by
Mastaprint Ltd, Nottingham

FLEXISCHOOLING

CONTENTS

Foreword	by James Hemming	viii
Preface		ix
Chapter one :	From Home-based Education to Flexischooling	1
Chapter two :	The Parents : An Agenda of Possibilities	11
Chapter three :	The Learners : A Wider Range of Pupil Roles	18
Chapter four :	The Teachers : A Repertoire of Roles	27
Chapter five :	Flexibility and the Curriculum	32
Chapter six :	Resources, Locations and Contracts : Schools as Learning Resource Centres	40
Chapter seven :	Conclusion : Education in a Changing Society.	49
Postscript	by Philip Toogood	54
References		61
Index		63

FOREWORD

AT PRESENT, in many forms, a tug-of-war is going on around the world between the authoritarians and the liberators. The authoritarians hold to a set of ideas and behaviours to which, they believe, others must be induced to submit. The liberators believe that, in any human situation, the most constructive outcome can only be reached by nourishing the unique powers of inherent in every person and group. The general purpose of the authoritarians is to maximise conformity; that of the liberators, to maximise creativity. The liberators seek an agreed order in running society - an order arising from the tasks and aims that need to be pursued. The authoritarians, in contrast, put their faith in imposed order. If order breaks down, the liberators response is to increase the intercommunication and uncover the underlying frustrations; the authoritarian answer is to increase the imposition and to pile penalties on those who will not comply.

There can be no doubt with which of these outlooks the future lies. The vast problems facing humankind today are not to be solved by rigid conformity but by releasing into effective growth and action every ounce of creativity we can mobilize.

Unfortunately, education, which should be the growing point for the future, is ridden by authoritarian approaches, in spite of the liberating efforts of individuals and groups who have sought to create educative environments in which children can grow in amicable relationships with their fellows and the adults around them. So it comes about that what is heralded as the Great Education Reform Bill of 1988 turns out to be yet another tactic for forcing children into preconceived patterns instead of nurturing their individual growth.

At such a time, it is vital that the alternatives should be explored. One of these is flexischooling, which fits well with the openness, variety and easy intercommunications which will increasingly characterize the way society operates. The child incarcerated in the classroom is not the right model for the contemporary world. But the mobile child exploring, at the same time, his/her own powers and the surrounding environment, which can be nothing less than the whole world, which flexischooling allows, is a more suitable model. We now know that personal fulfilment and personal participation in affairs are both essential aspects of individual growth. Education must operate through these dynamics.

Roland Meighan has, for many years, been working at liberating prospective teachers, experienced teachers, and parents and their children from the dead hand of authoritarianism in education. We do well to study closely what he has to say. It gives us a pattern for a way ahead that could transform education.

James Hemming   Ph.D., B.A., F.B.Ps.S., F.R.S.A.

July 1988

PREFACE

Education is subject to considerable ironies. In 1988, as one country (Denmark) invests £38 million pounds in a four year experiment to develop the school of the future, another (U.K.) implements the old idea much favoured by socialists in the 1950's, of a National Curriculum, claiming that it is part of the master plan to 'bury socialism'. In another country, the U.S.A., the National Board Association produces a report entitled "Technology and the Transformation of Schools" which forecasts that the school will become just part of a total approach to learning, linked to the home, the community and its workplaces, and the whole environment of the learners. The role of teachers as instructors will become minor as computers, laser discs, telecommunications and interactive robotics take up such functions. However, the role of "learning professionals" who can counsel and guide students through the technology and the learning networks, will expand. Lewis Perelman, who prepared the report, states that "those that resist change risk following the downhill path blazed by America's giant steel companies."

A selection of comments by headteachers in the U.K. suggests that something is being overlooked by those who seem to think that the present model of school is a sound enough foundation to build on:

"Schools could become as obsolete as steam trains or paddle steamers"
    C.Everett at the Public Schools Headmasters Conference 1987

"Deep in my bones I remain convinced that ultimately it will be the de-schoolers who are proved right, and that far in the future our descendants will view the whole concept of the school with mirth and disbelief."
    Gerald Haigh

"The justification for school in its present form no longer exists."
    Philip Toogood

Another irony of education is illustrated by the attitudes of adults in power positions who have consistently made such an appalling mess of the world and its societies. They continue relentlessly to act in the same tradition, confidently prescribing education systems that constrain children to become similar people to them ! Carl Rogers writing about the situation in the U.S.A. has this to say about such systems :

"Our educational system is, I believe, failing to meet the real needs of our society. I have said that our schools, generally, constitute the most traditional, conservative, rigid, bureaucratic institution of our time, and the institution most resistant to change."

Rogers seems to side with Oscar Wilde in his view that the longer he lived, the more keenly he felt that whatever was good enough for our fathers was definitely not good enough for us.

One writer, Everett Reimer, gave his verdict on the education system thus :

"Some true education experiences are bound to occur in schools. They occur, however, despite school and not because of it."

A number of educationalists, including myself, who agree with the general drift of Reimer's observation, might have some reservations, e.g. that this is less true of most early childhood education in the U.K. than it is of most secondary education. Furthermore, those of us who think that the present government's ideas in education are moribund and jejune and are likely to decrease the likelihood of true educational experiences occurring in schools even further, have a responsibility to outline something better. (The previous Labour government was equally regressive in educational ideas, so I am not making a party political observation here.) This book is an attempt to discharge that responsibility.

I must acknowledge a considerable debt to a whole variety of educational trailblazers. These include the hundreds of parents in Education Otherwise that I have been privileged to meet, and occasionally to defend in court, teachers involved in the Community Education Movement, the staff and pupils of innovative state and private schools, members of the recently formed Education on a Human Scale group, and the many pupils, students, colleagues, friends, and writers who have contributed ideas and reactions to my teaching and research over the years. Regular contact with educationalists in U.S.A., Australia, Sweden and various other countries have also been influential.

I owe an enormous debt of gratitude to Janet, who like Jeeves in Bertie Wooster's words of admiration, stands alone.

Also appreciation is due to James, who stuck to his own judgment and chose to go to school managing, in his own words, to continue to rescue bits from the wreck, and thus helped me keep my mind open. I should like to thank Ron Biggs, Gerald Cortis, James Hemming, Robert Shayler, Jonathon Sherlock and Philip Toogood for their invaluable support and comments on the manuscript. (Additional and unsponsored thanks are due to Amstrad for the amazing PCW 8256 Word Processor.)

Roland Meighan

Chapter One.

From Home-based Education to Flexischooling?

"I believe that the computer presence will enable us so to modify the learning environment outside the classroom, that much, if not all the knowledge schools presently try to teach with such pains and expense and such limited success will be learned, as the child learns to talk, painlessly, successfully, and without organised instruction.
This obviously implies that schools, as we know them today, will have no place in the future. But it is an open question whether they will adapt by transforming themselves into something new or wither away and be replaced."
Seymour Papert in *Mindstorms, Children, Computers, and Powerful Ideas.*

The Experience of Home-based Education.

In 1976 a new educational organisation was set up entitled Education Otherwise. It was a small self-help and mutual support group for a handful of families, about a dozen, who were educating their children at home in preference to sending them to school. The name of the organisation was taken from the 1944 Education Act which laid a primary responsibility on parents to ensure that their children were educated 'either by regular attendance at school or otherwise.'

My involvement with this group became threefold. Firstly, there was a rare opportunity to research an educational group from its launching. Secondly, my own child was nearing school age and both parents had decided to make school optional and not compulsory by offering home-based education to him as an alternative. Thirdly, having become an active member and supporter of this group, there was the task of helping families establish their rights in court cases. I undertook the role of 'expert witness' on several occasions.

Education Otherwise grew in size and its current roll is over a thousand families. During this growth, the research showed one regular feature. The large majority of families involved did not actually want to educate their children at home. They were forced into it by frustration and desperation. They were desperate that their children were not doing well at school, were unhappy, not sleeping at night, so that the family was in turmoil. They became so desperate that they clutched at the last possible straw of trying to educate their children at home.

After some experience of home-based education most were well pleased with their decision and saw it as the best educational option available. Nevertheless, most could also imagine a better option still - that of a part-time arrangement with a local school. What they were looking for was a kind of shared responsibility, an educational contract and partnership.

It is not the case that families undertaking home-based education are particularly anti-school. Some families opt into the system again at various stages. There are all sorts of patterns. I have come across families who have educated their children at home until they reach the age of eleven and then opted into the secondary school, and other families who have done exactly the reverse. Some families actually have one child in school and one out of school. The one out may be planning to go back sometime in the future, whilst the one in can be considering the possibility of a phase of home-based education being built into their future plans.

The Local Education Authorities have been known to say, "Why can't you make up your mind? Are you in favour of schools or aren't you?" The families say, " We are not against school or for school. We are in favour of education and if education for this child is best done at home for now, then that is where we do it. If for this child it is best done at school for now, then that is where we do it. We are perfectly consistent. We are for what works best for this learner at this time." The families demonstrate a capacity for flexibility which contrasts with the rigidity of schooling as currently practised. They are already pointing the way to the notion of "flexischooling".

Flexischooling is the word used to describe this notion of a part-time arrangement whereby school and family sharing responsibility in an agreed contract and partnership. Later it took on other layers of meaning as we shall see. The term first emerged in conversations I enjoyed with the late John Holt, the writer and educationalist from the U.S.A. Before his death in 1986, John Holt wrote many notable eduational books such as *How Children Fail*. His final book was *Teach Your Own* for in his last years he devoted his time and efforts to home-based education in his country in association with the organisation Growing Without Schooling.

Flexischooling.

This apparently simple notion quickly began to develop a number of layers of meaning. Flexischooling, even in its first formulations, could be seen to be based on rather different assumptions from those of schooling in Britain in the 1970's:

- there does not have to be a single location for education. There can be several, including schools, homes, work-places, museums and libraries.

- parents are not defined as part of the problems of education but as part of the solutions for they are seen as having an active educational role in cooperation and partnership with schools.

- children can learn without a teacher being present. This comes as no surprise to Correspondence Colleges or the Word-wide Education Service with over a hundred years of experience in helping expatriate families educate their children in foreign countries.

- teaching is not synonymous with instructing. Other activities, either initiated by others for learners, such as organising a simulation, or in response to the initiatives of learners, such as helping them locate resources to further their own research, are types of teaching. Thus, facilitating learning is a teaching act as well as 'full frontal' instruction. If this were not so the Open University tutors who write course units for students they may never meet are receiving their salaries under false pretences.

- resources available at home can be utilized in educational programmes. These include the ubiquitous T.V. and radio, as well as cassette recorders, video recorders, and home computers where they are available.

In its later expanded formulations, flexischooling, seen more generally as a much more flexible approach to education in all its dimensions, raises more questions still. For example, could the curriculum become a negotiated experience instead of an imposed one? Could there be choice from the variety of types of curriculum available? In general it offers the prospect of diversifying from the present base of educational practices, without jettisoning the more positive features. It would be foolish, for instance, to write off many of the initiatives which have occurred in nursery and early childhood schooling in Britain which are still admired and emulated by visitors from abroad.

Recent Innovations in Schools.

It would also be foolish to pretend that the features listed above were entirely absent from the current scene. In each case there are initiatives in some parts of the schooling system. As regards location, the Open University has pioneered the use of homes, of self help groups meeting in the members' own chosen locations, and of buildings in the community for study centre meetings. In schools the older pupils are often encouraged to work at home, especially just before examinations, and most Local Education Authorities have a home teaching service used for a variety of purposes. The Manpower Services Commission (MSC) in various projects such as the Technical and Vocational Initiative (TVEI) and the Youth Training Scheme (YTS) has concentrated on the use of workplaces as a location for learning.

As regards the role of parents, one primary school in Oxfordshire has experimented with home-based work for one afternoon a week for parents who wish to make use of such an opportunity (see North 1987). Perhaps the most sustained work has been done in Coventry where the Community Development Project has developed a wide range of initiatives involving parents in an educational role since the mid 1970's.

That children can learn without a teacher always being present is a commonplace with correspondence colleges and the World-wide Education Service but has also been the experience of the members of Education Otherwise when they have developed their educational programmes at home. But schools can also claim some experience of this kind. The Schools Council General Studies Project, though only partially successful, was an initiative in individualised learning through purpose designed study units that could operate with or without teachers being present.

The idea that teaching is confined to formal instruction has also been questioned particularly in early childhood education and again in the development of learning strategies such as games and simulations in secondary schools. Some teachers in some schools have tried to incorporate the resources available at home, newspapers, T.V., etc., in devising homework activities.

It is clear, however, that these are not standard practices nor are they accepted as part of the orthodoxy of schooling. The schools involved are often flying in the face of accepted practice and risking consequent ridicule. It is not without significance that when my son's request for a flexischooling arrangement was being considered, the headteacher responded to the proposition that he might become hailed as an educational pioneer, with, "Pioneer? I'm more likely to become an educational martyr!"

Schooling is Currently Based on an Outdated Model.

Many of the inflexibilities of contemporary schooling in Britain have their roots in the thinking of the past. The conditions in which mass schooling was established, just over a hundred years ago, led to practices that made sense at the time but have now been taken over by events. The case of the role of parents illustrates the phenomenon. In 1870 the assumption was made that most of the parents were illiterate and ill-informed and that education was best put solely in the hands of trained teachers. In the 1980's the partial success of the schooling system means that most parents are literate, many are well qualified, some are better qualified than teachers, and most better informed than before, not least because of regular contact with the mass media. Furthermore, many have a wider experience of life than the majority of teachers who have completed the tight circle from school to university or college, and back into school.

Some of the ideas adopted in 1870 have older roots still. Hemming (1980) notes that the ideas of modern psychology about brain functioning and learning are still overlooked in favour of more ancient and fallacious ideas:

" It is an extraordinary fact that the dominant influences operating in secondary education have no scientific basis whatever. They arise from dubitable philosophical ideas that had their origin in the distant past - the Greek view that the craftsman was inherently inferior to the thinker; Locke's presentation of the mind as a clean slate, as a tabula rasa; Descartes' over-evaluation of the intellect, and his division of the human being into mind (exalted) and body (debased); puritan ideas about the special value of making the young do what they don't like doing."

A similar point is made by Husen (1974) when he argues that the basic assumptions underlying schooling as it tends to be practised are all dubious and rooted in past-orientated ideas. These assumptions are that people will learn only if motivated by the avoidance of disagreeable consequences, that what learners can achieve is rationed by something known as ability, and that tasks based on textbooks indicate the best and highest forms of 'ability'. Until these fallacious ideas are abandoned, Husen and Hemming see schools as continuing to limit the development of young people.

The group of writers rather misleadingly known as the deschoolers,(since they were for the most part in favour of regenerating schooling rather than abandoning it altogether), were prone to describe the consequences of schooling in these terms:

" the students who endure it come out as passive, acquiescent, dogmatic, *intolerant, authoritarian, inflexible, conservative personalities who desperately need to resist change in an effort to keep their illusion of certainty intact.*"
(*Postman and Weingartner 1971*)

In contrast, parents in Education Otherwise who opt for an autonomous approach in their home-based educational programmes stress self education, personal confidence, problem solving, flexibility and adaptation and see their task as liberating their children from some of the effects Postman and Weingartner postulate.

Inflexibility in the Present System.

If in its more developed formulations, flexischooling can be seen as making schooling much more flexible in a whole variety of ways, what are the rigidities that are in question? They derive from operating one ideology of education as if it were the one right way rather than as one of several existing alternatives. An ideology of education (or a philosophy of education, or a vision of education, if you prefer,) is seen here as a set of component 'theories' that lead people to try to teach and learn in particular ways. Thus, to take Husen's proposition that schooling has been based on what he sees as a fallacious theory of learning, (that pupils are, for the most part, to be motivated by the avoidance of disagreeable consequences), the outcome will be a programme that stresses imposed order, control by adults and the use of punishments. School will be analagous to the organisation of an army. It will be coercive rather than cooperative or negotiated.

The rigidities of the present system of schooling in the U.K. can be classified in various ways. Here I will attempt to examine them by looking at the component theories that go to make up a particular ideology of education.

(a) *Theory of Knowledge*

Knowledge may be interpreted as being predominately past-orientated, present-orientated, or future-orientated. In the first view, heavy reliance will be placed on the ancient subject divisions devised by our ancestors. In the second, views of the need to devise integrated forms of knowledge are proposed on the grounds that complex modern concerns like pollution, mass media, computer technology, terrorism, and education are cross-disciplinary and in need of new information and ideas to cope with them. The third view stresses the need for learners to concentrate on the acquisition of learning skills to cope with a future in which knowledge is continuously expanding and changing and to gain the confidence to use these skills in any situation in which they may find themselves. (The celebration of the first view is seen in almost any secondary school timetable where, like the cuckoo, subjects have managed to eject the eggs of anything else that might have been laid in early childhood education, out of the nest.)

(b) *Theory of Learning*

Learning may be viewed as a collective activity best organised in large groups of thirty or more, or a more intimate activity best organised in small groups not exceeding twelve, or as predominately an individual activity. It may be seen as a competitive activity, one learner against another, or as a cooperative activity, or as a personal development against criteria of achievement. Learning can be seen as motivated by the avoidance of disagreeable consequences like low marks, censure and punishment, or as an inevitable feature of human consciousness unless discouraged. Learning is believed to be achieved through listening, or alternatively through visual means, or through doing or active participation. The appropriate outcomes of education can be held to be, in turn, believing, memorising, critical thinking, or skills acquistion.

By the time pupils have settled into secondary school in the U.K. they are usually experiencing the first set of all these options i.e. working in large groups, under threat of sanctions, competing for marks, listening for long periods of time, with the outcomes of memorising or believing conventional doctrines. The enthusiasm, activity and involvement of earlier years is rarely in evidence.

(c) *Theory of Teaching*

Teaching may be seen as the giving of formal instruction, or as the facilitation of learning through organising learning situations, or as self-teaching through undertaking the organising of learning situations oneself. Thus the expertise claimed for the teacher's role can be of several kinds. It can be based on the skills in instructing others in a given subject. Alternatively it can be based on expertise in organising learning - an educational technology or learning systems approach. A third possibility is that of learning consultant where the teacher responds to the initiatives of the learners for instruction, advice on learning systems, or whatever counselling is appropriate. In this last case the teacher is closest to being in loco parentis since this has been shown to be the method used by parents to teach their children to talk. The activity of teachers may stress product or process, requiring in the first case getting learners to give right or required answers and in the second to develop strategies of thinking. By the time pupils have completed their years of compulsory education in the U.K. most will have become habituated to teaching as instruction stressing the product of supplying the required answers.

(d)*Theory of Parents*

The role of the parent can be seen in different ways. In one view, parents are problems to be dealt with by the professionally trained teachers. Alternatively, they are clients who should control the activity of potentially wayward teachers through governing bodies. In another view, they are para-professional aides who can be useful to teachers. Next they may be seen as partners with teachers working to agreed schedules. In the rarest view, parents are the primary educators who may or may not decide to involve teachers in their educational programme.

The first role definition of parents as problems, whether interferers or neglectful or something else, has been predominant since the 1870's when mass schooling was established. Since most parents were then assumed to be illiterate with no experience of schooling, it was thought that education was best left to the professionals. As schooling has been partially successful the other definitions of the parent's role have been emerging with growing but irregular frequency, often with strong opposition from schools.

(e) *Theory of Resources*

Resources may be teachers, books, television, radio, film, magazines, newspapers, people, places and experiences. Where books are seen as predominant, there will be a school library, perhaps class libraries and subject book storerooms. If multi-media resources are thought desirable, then school resources centres may develop. If people, places and experiences are seen as prime sources of learning, then the whole environment of learners in and out of schools will be utilised.

Resources may be made available to learners in varying degrees of access. They may be limited by access available only through a teacher, or largely limited to one sex, (e.g. home economics) or to one age group, or to insiders only. The community education movement, for instance, operates on the assumption that both insiders and outsiders should have access to some of the resources of the school. Open access to resources is another possibility as in the case of a public library.

Schools differ in the emphasis placed on first-hand, second-hand and third-hand experiences as resources for learning. As schooling progresses, textbooks, where writers summarise what people other than the writer have done, thought or experienced for the learner to encounter at third hand, may become predominant as the pressure for written examination results builds.

(f) *Theory of Location*

Learning may be seen as best undertaken in a special building which may be a school, a college or university. Alternatively it may be undertaken in a community operating from an organisational base as in the case of the 'anywhere' or 'everywhere' or 'street' schools that have been experimented with in the U.S.A. (e.g. the Parkway Project in Philadelphia) Or learning may be organised using home as a base as in the case of the Open University or Education Otherwise families. In another view, the City as School in New York has defined workplaces as the central focus for high school pupils and a succession of work experiences makes up the core of the curriculum.

(e) *Theory of Organisation*

The general organisation of a school may be seen as the headteacher's task. It can be seen as a senior management team's responsibility. Alternatively, it is a whole staff concern. Sometimes it is defined as the concern of the whole learning community involving pupils too. More rarely it is thought to be the task of the whole community including parents, employers as well as school cleaners and caretakers. A governing body may be seen as the responsible group. Alternatively, the key organisational device may be seen as a contract between learners, teachers and parents, requiring negotiation and regular review.

From the key decision about power and responsibility the other detailed decisions about the organisation of time, the curriculum, rules and records are likely to develop. Ironically, in what is held to be a democracy, schools have been required to perpetuate the rigid models of organisation found in more totalitarian or religiously fanatical countries, and to ignore the more flexible forms of order and organisation available that have developed since the 1870's. School organisation can be seen to be anachronistic, yet those schools that have tried to get away from coercive organisational forms have been subjected to trial by tabloid journalism.

(f) *Theory of Assessment*

The view of who is the most appropriate person to assess varies from the external examiner of an examination board, to the teachers of a set of learners, to prospective employers, to the learners themselves. What should be assessed is also subject to rival interpretations. For some, the courses should be assessed for their efficiency as learning experiences. For others, the teachers should be appraised for their efficiency as instructors. For yet others, the learners should be examined for their achievements as learners. The purpose in mind varies : assessment may be seen as diagnostic to direct further learning, or as selective to sort out who is worthy for the prize of a job, or a university place, or as indicative to identify an achievement profile at a particular time.

The focus may be on written performances, on practical skills, on conversation and discussion skills, on the processes of learning, adapting, revising and thinking, or on the end products of memory tests. The form of assessment may vary from references, to reports, to record cards, to folders of work, to porfolios, to personal files, to profiles , to certificates, to self-report schedules. Schools currently find themselves limited to being judged on a rigid and highly suspect theory of assessment, that of external examination.

Which theory dominates has financial as well as psychological and educational significance. Thus one European country, Sweden, abandoned external school examinations as outdated over thirty five years ago and saved large sums of money by disbanding all their expensive examination boards. Since this money was spent on resourcing the schools instead, the result, judged both by my regular visits and observations, as well as the attempted international comparisons of achievement, is a much higher standard of education than that of the U.K.

(g)*Theory of Aims*

The society for which education is thought to be preparing pupils can be characterised in various ways. It may be seen as a society of rigid inequality where pupils are eventually allocated to occupational roles according to birth or patronage. It may be seen as a state of fluidity with mobility for a minority based on some means of competition and selection. Other visions of society stress some form of equality. Another alternative proposes a pluralistic society with conflicts of interest resolved by democratic means. These do not exhaust the possibilities. The aims given most priority vary according to which vision of society is being promoted and they will be selected from an agenda that includes the following :
Education should aim at :
    preparation for living out the prescriptions of a particular religion
    preparation for personal autonomy and personal development
    producing people who will serve the needs of the economy
    preparation for constructive leisure
    producing people who will be participating citizens in a democracy
    preparation for economic activity as a consumer
    developing people who will conform to the society as it is
    producing people who will change society through research and innovation
    preparing citizens who are capable of adapting to changes that occur in an uncertain future
    producing people who will serve their nation without question
    preparing people for an increasingly international identity

According to which order of priority these are given in a nation, and which are excluded, we can begin to classify that country as being predominately fascist, religious fundamentalist, nationalist, democratic, pluralistic, totalitarian, communist, capitalist, or some combination of these such as welfare capitalist. There are other possibilities still e.g.internationalist. In the U.K. the nationalist-economic and conformist aims appear to be held as paramount and this rather limited vision can be seen as contributing to the rigidity of the present system.

Conclusion

These component theories of education are given only in outline here, and I have dealt with them in more detail elsewhere (Meighan 1986). Research students have used them and developed them further in various investigative studies. They serve to draw attention to the complex sources of rigidity within an education system and to show that becoming more flexible in educational practice is a multidimensional problem. The next three chapters focus on three key possibilities for becoming more flexible: the roles of parents, the roles of learners, and the roles of teachers.

Chapter Two

The Parents - An Agenda of Possibilities

"Perhaps in the not too distant future, man's intelligence will have improved so much that children will be able to be taught by their parents in their home."
Jennifer in *The School That I'd Like* edited by Edward Blishen

An Education System That Has Not Adjusted To Its Own Success

When mass schooling was established in 1870 in the U.K., parents were more or less excluded from consideration since most were assumed to be illiterate. The majority had not received any formalised education themselves and they were not necessarily ecpected to be sympathetic to the new arrangements. Instead, it was claimed that education was best left to the 'professionals', the body of teachers that the government would train and license. The role of parent was seen as that of spectator, admiring or otherwise. The other potential definition was that of parent as problem, either because they did not or could not do the expected minimum in the way of physical preparation for school attendance and were deemed 'neglectful', or because they took too lively an interest in what was going on and could be identified as 'interferers'.

That the state should organise mass schooling was not the only option. The Chartists appeared to favour state support for the development of the existing pattern in all its variety, which was based on the work of educational pioneers, voluntary groups, churches, and parents, in preference to any regimentalised state takeover. Charlotte Mason saw parents as having a legitimate educational role, and she was involved in both school-based and home-based versions of eduation as we shall see. But the general approach of parental exclusion prevailed.

Over a hundred years later, these conditions have changed in various ways. The education system has been partially successful since most parents are now literate, and the majority have been pupils in the system themselves thus having had an experience of formal education. They have also been subject to a new and rival education influence in the form of the mass media, in particular television but also radio and mass circulation magazines and newspapers. One feature of this has been the growth of a market for books for parents to buy and use at home to augment or complement school based activity.

Has the education system has responded to the changing situation by re-defining the role of parents? The verdict appears to be 'not much'. The phenomenon of culture inertia appears to be in evidence whereby one institution fails to adapt to changes in the others. The attitude of one Primary school headteacher of, " All I ask of parents is that they should bring it to school clean and well-dressed......I shall do the rest, " is still commonplace, though currently it is under pressure from initiatives that carve out some involvement for parents who desire it.

There would appear to be a range of definitions of the role of parents currently operating in the U.K. :
Parent as Problem
Parent as Police
Parent as Para-Professional Aide
Parent as Partner
Parent as Pre-school Educator
Parent as the Prime Educator
These are listed roughly in order of flexibility so that if it is possible to identify which type is dominant in a particular school, we have some idea where it lies in respect of flexischooling in this specific dimension. It remains to explain what each of these definitions implies.

Parent as Problem

The general theory that parents present a problem remains current today. The task for those schools operating with this view is to diagnose which kind of problem parent is being presented. Is it an interferer or a neglecter or is it one that can be neutralised into a spectator, admiring or otherwise. The study by Sharp and Green (1975) indicated some of the procedures and their consequences. Four features of the 'good' parent were noted.
(a) Parents need to be well informed about the way the school operates and its ideology of education.
(b) Parents need to demonstrate a strong interest in the education of their children and have motivation for their success.
(c) The school's view of what constitutes 'good' parents needs to be read accurately by the parents concerned.
(d) The impression has to be managed that the parents accept and support the school's views.
The relationship with the school can become negative if any of these features is missing. Yet in the case of the first requirement, obtaining reliable information is not easy even assuming that the school is actually consistent in its behaviour. The sources of information - visits to school initiated meetings, impressions from children, clues from work brought home, talking with other parents - are all subject to ambiguity and parents can develop varying degrees of confusion. The more confusion, the more misinterpretation that is possible.

In the case of the second feature, parents vary in their view of an appropriate education. Sharp and Green found that although all expressed some degree of concern for the development of reading, writing and numeracy, some put an even higher priority on general happiness. Others valued a broad curriculum with creative and artistic activities given a high prominence. Because of these variations, some parents would find it easy to connect with the particular view operationing in the local school, while others may stand back in a state of reluctant tolerance and be seen as 'apathetic'.

The third and fourth features were seen to be crucial. Parents vary in their reading of the school's definition of 'good' parents as well as their subsequent reactions. Some fail in collecting sufficient reliable information about the school and can easily fall into the trap of being seen as neglectful. Others take too keen an interest, becoming 'interferers'. Some decide to be admiring spectators, only to be seen as apathetic. (Teachers who are also parents may well have experienced, as I have, the ritual of evenings for parents where a teacher has been striving for clues to diagnose which label to fix on me as the parent in question.) The 'good' parent does not need to be well informed or in agreement with the school's ideology, only to manage the impression that this is the case. The successful parents, in terms of having children who are successful at the school, avoid the label of interferers while actually interfering persistently behind the scenes by teaching their children to read, write and develop numeracy at home, for if they did not their children are likely to fall behind those whose parents were. There are several ironies here. If parents actually operate on the definition of good parent their children are at risk of falling behind. The staff think it is their activity that makes the difference whereas it is the clandestine activity or lack of it by parents that is probably responsible. Furthermore, those parents most in favour at the school are those who, in their actual behind-the-scenes behaviour, imply, without articulating it, a sustained criticism of the school regime.

Parent as Police

If the education system is publicly perceived as inadequate, it can become politically expedient to define teachers as the problem. One response is to maintain that the teachers need to be made to be responsible to parents by putting the parents in charge. The government Green Paper on parents (1984) takes this view and proposes that parents take charge by having an overall majority on school governing bodies, thus being able to police the activities of the school and its staff. That similar arrangements do not exist for the police force, the medical profession or the legal profession is pertinent here. Specifically, a small minority of parents can seize power in this situation and dictate their preferences to both school and other parents and this is therefore a potentially limiting and stultifying development in the role of parent and likely to be anti-democratic in consequence.

Parent as Para-professional Aide

When parents begin to be considered as part of the solution rather than defined as part of the problem, one response is to experiment with parents as resources for the school and its teachers. The most sustained efforts appear to have been made in Coventry under the umbrella of the Community Education Centre. A report on the effects of involving parents in the educational programme of primary schools in Coventry was entitled Raising Standards (Widlake and Macleod 1984). It demonstrated that children from less privileged backgrounds were not necessarily doomed to fail but could improve their performance when parents were included rather than excluded from the educational team.

The practise of involving parents in the teaching of reading has been increasing in U.K. primary schools. The Haringey Project based in an inner city area in London was the subject of close scrutiny. One researcher, Hewison, concluded that the project showed that most parents in the area were willing as well as competent to help their children learn to read under the direction of the school. In another part of the country, the Belfield Project at Rochdale yielded similar results, as did the Fox Hill Reading Workshop in Sheffield. As the barriers break down, both parties learn a new respect for each other. From the Fox Hill Reading Workshop, a parent remarks, 'I understand better what a teacher has to cope with having to teach children.' A teacher admiring the activity of the parents and its efficacy, says, ' They could have done all this before ,but we didn't know.'

In all these instances, the school and its teachers take the initiative and encourage parents to assist largely on the school's terms for school defined ends and to become aides to the enterprise of the 'professionals'. The more flexible approach to the contribution of parents that this represents can be distinguished from situations where the parents become closer to being equal partners.

Parent as Partner

One project with a hundred years of experience of parents as partners in the education of their children is the World-wide Educational Service (WES) of the Parent's National Education Union which was founded by Charlotte Mason. Although correspondence is a central feature of the WES scheme, it is not strictly speaking a correspondence course but something more flexible. The programmes,the tutors and the parents operate in partnership. Usually the family concerned comes to the WES headquarters for a consultation to meet their tutor and assess and locate the appropriate programme. Required books can be purchased on the spot so that a family can depart fully equipped to start, knowing that they can contact their tutor whenever they need to as well as send in work produced at regular intervals for sympathetic assessment. The programmes are schemes of work explaining to parents how to set up and run their home-based education using the materials supplied as a basis, as well as how they can adapt and develop additional initiatives of their own. The programmes have Department of Education and Science endorsement and their success over the hundred years with thousands of families all over the world is well established.

The parent is seen as in partnership with the tutor and the programmes provided, using the style of operation Charlotte Mason described as 'masterful inactivity' (Boulter 1984). This does not signal that the parent does nothing. They have been rather busy facilitating the whole enterprise in any case. Instead, it stresses that the learners should now be allowed to get on with learning with the minimum of interference or interruption and without presupposing precise outcomes. The key elements in the act of 'teaching' are seen as providing the raw materials and encouraging interest and enthusiasm. Whilst the mere presence of the parent acts as a control even though he or she appears to do nothing specific, the learner produces his or her own work, not a restricted aping of the parent's ideas or the programme writer's notions.

The WES is not only concerned with home-based education but with a range of consultancy and support services to schools. The same concept of parents as active partners in the educational process informs the work here too . The WES is not, therefore, for or against schools but in favour of variety and choice in educational practice and .
".....has little patience either with the arid, defensive professionalism of a minority of teachers who think that they alone can educate children or with those parents who seem to be opposed to all schools per se." (Boulter 1984)

It is of some significance that the parent takes the initiative in approaching WES and then agrees to an informal contract to take a central part as an active partner in the programme that develops. This is in contrast to the Para-professional Aide role where the initiatives are controlled by the school staff and can be collapsed by them.

Parent as Pre-school Educator

The education of children for the first five years of their life is largely in the hands of their parents. There are a few exceptions in the case of children brought up in institutional care. Parents have been instrumental in helping their children learn all the things they are able to do before they set foot in a school. In the case of learning to speak the mother tongue, this is no mean accomplishment, given that a new-born baby has a spoken language achievement of precisely nil. The methods used are informal, avoiding set instructional modes in a style Waterland (1985) describes as the apprenticeship approach. Some of the impressive detail of the work of parents is documented in the research of Wells (1985) who followed a representative sample of children in Bristol from fifteen months to the age of ten. Virtually all the children were at least competent conversationalists by the age of five and some very accomplished. The children with lower achievement were limited by the quality of their talk with the adults around them and this was a feature of the transfer into school where the quality of talk went down. Transcripts showed that parents tended to respond sensitively to their children's interests, expanding their contributions and feeding in relevant ideas and information. The children's conversations in school with teachers were of lower quality with a pre-set agenda in operation and limited responses to the children's contributions and concerns. Wells sees this as related to the unreasonable workloads, group sizes and conditions of work rather than teacher incompetence. Waterland is in favour of continuing to utilise the skills of parents as educators in the development of reading, in partnership with teachers in the 'apprenticeship' approach. The work of parents in the first five years is seen as being augmented and amplified by school rather than substituted or taken over.

Parent as the Prime Educator

Parents are the prime educators in most cases up until their children are five years of age. If they choose to involve the use of play groups or nursery schools or some other source of assistance it is by their decision and they retain the right to end any such arrangements. In contrast, when their children start school at five, control moves into the hands of the education system and its staff.

A few parents prefer to retain control and remain the prime educator by taking up their option in law to educate at home since it is education that is required by law not schooling per se. Parents are given the right to discharge their legal obligation to ensure that their children receive an adequate education 'either by attendance at school or otherwise.' A mutual aid and support group entitled Education Otherwise was set up in the U.K. in 1976 and the number of families involved has grown from an initial dozen or so to over two thousand. An equivalent organisation, Growing Without Schooling, has been established in the U.S.A. for about the same length of time and is also expanding at a similar rate with the energetic support of John Holt until his death in 1986. (see Holt,J. *Teach Your Own* published in 1984.)

Most of the first wave of parents who decided to develop a home-based educational alternative were motivated by desperation because their children were so unhappy at school, or achieving little, or both. A second group of parents who are able to articulate their views on the harmful effects of schooling and are well informed about research on the hidden curriculum of mass education have increased from a small minority to a large grouping within Education Otherwise. These parents decide to remain the prime educators and to continue the work they have begun in the first five years with a home-based educational programme. In principle this is not a new idea and, as was noted earlier, the World-wide Educational Service has supported parents in such ventures for over a hundred years.

Famous people such as Yehudi Menuhin and Margaret Mead and less famous but successful people have been educated at home. What is new is that this approach was successfully adopted by families of modest means and modest social standing who found that, with energy and imagination, they could match and then overtake, in most respects, the quality of education available in schools. One family excited by its success published its experience under the title, "Anything School Can Do You Can Do Better." On the evidence available, a caveat of 'with only a few exceptions' might have increased the modesty as well as the accuracy of the title.

The majority of parents in Education Otherwise, however, are not dogmatically opposed to school. The wish to have cooperative links with the local school that their taxes pay for, is commonly expressed. Although home-based education is seen as the best available option, most parents can envisage an even better option, a flexible, cooperative programme with home and school working in an agreed partnership . It was from this response in both the U.K. and the U.S.A. that in conversations the writer had with John Holt, the concept of flexischooling began to be explored.

The role of the parent in the case of home-based education remains that of the prime educator. Many families decide to opt in to the education system at various stages and then out again according to their needs as they define them. Education officials have sometimes expressed exasperation and asked families to make up their minds whether they are for school or against, to which the reply has been that they were neither for against schools , but in favour of education in whatever form worked for a particular child at a particular time. These parents operate a form of flexischooling already, but one limited to large blocks of time in one place or another rather than a flexible use of locations.

Conclusion.

The six roles examined above may not be the only possible categorisations but they serve to make the point that some role definitions are rigid and limiting and others more flexible and developmental. It is by developing the latter that flexischooling can become a reality in the particular dimension of the parent role.

The experience of those who have been operating with the more flexible role definitions for parents is that there can be a significant by-product. Parents who become involved in educational activity in partnership with schools can find a re-awakening of interest in their own education. Schools can find themselves dealing with requests to run classes for parents, or for parents to join senior classes as learners, or to give advice on National Extension College courses, the Open University and other forms of further education.

Chapter Three

The Learners : A Wider Range of Pupil Roles

"Education is an admirable thing but it is well to remember from time to time that nothing that is worth knowing can be taught."
Oscar Wilde in *The Critic as Artist*.

Learning and the Knowledge Explosion.

In 1858 the view of learning that was acceptable was expressed by James Fraser, later to become Bishop of Manchester, to the Newcastle Commission :
"....*I venture to maintain that it is quite possible to teach a child soundly and thoroughly, in a way that he shall not forget it, all that is necessary for him to possess in the shape of intellectual attainment, by the time that he is ten years old.*".

In the hundred and twenty or so years since this view was current, there have been a few changes. Not least amongst these is what has been identified as the knowledge explosion. Information is seen to be increasing rapidly, perhaps doubling every ten years. The means of distributing this information, the mass media, have also arrived on the scene along with the technology of computers and communications by satellite. Some of the features of this radically changed situation are outlined in these observations by North (1982):

"We no longer have to force-feed education to children : they live in a world in which they are surrounded by educative resources.

There are around five hundred hours each of the schools' television and radio every year in this country. There are several million books in public libraries. There are museums in every town. There is a constant stream of cheap or free information from a dozen media. There are home computers which will soon be easily connected to phones and thus other computers.

There are thousands of work-places which are, or could be made, convenient for children, where they could learn about the reality of working lives and join in them. There are, as there have always been, the old, the disabled, the very young, all in need of children in their lives, all in need of the kind of help caring and careful youngsters can give, and all of them rich sources of information about the world, and freely available to any child who isn't locked away in a school."

The view of learning as the receiving, through direct instruction, of what is already known and in the memory or within the possession of the teacher, can still be encountered. Yet the implications of the knowledge and communications explosions mean that a teacher, or even a team of specialist teachers, cannot make any such claim - for the present and certainly not for the future. The knowledge of the even the most freshly trained teacher is quickly out of date. If the problems and information of the future cannot be forecast, then the emphasis must shift towards acquiring learning skills which are less likely to date. Watts (1980) lists some of these skills :

" ....it is crucial that the student learns in school: (a) how to identify a problem (whereas in a closed class the problem is always posed by the teacher);(b) how to plan a strategy for solving the problem (instead of a teacher detailing the method); (c) how to select and retrieve the information necessary for this problem-solving strategy; (d) how to derive hypotheses from this data - i.e. logical processes; (e) how to test hypotheses."

Watts adds to this list a role for imaginative speculation and the consideration of alternatives.

There is a variety of role definitions for learners to be found in operation in the U.K. They include the following:
1. Learner as Resister
2. Learner as Receptacle.
3. Learner as Raw Material
4. Learner as Client
5. Learner as Partner
6. Learner as Autonomous Explorer
7. Learner as Democratic Explorer

As in the case of the role variation for parents, these are given in an approximate order of flexibility, thus making it possible to note which type is dominant in a given school. From this it might be plausible to suggest where it might lie in respect of flexischooling in the dimension of learner roles for pupils. The most flexible situation would perhaps allow some function for all the learner definitions, although the first three could be seen as preferably becoming increasingly minor in incidence, and having a temporary role rather than a permanent place, in the light of the analysis by Watts above.

Learner as Resister

Holt (1984) writes of how he began to confront in his own thinking about education the view of learner as resister. At one of his lectures to an audience of American teachers outlining the familiar ideas of his as to how children learn to fail, one harsh, angry voice demanded to know what you did with the children who are just plain lazy. Holt recalls how the audience that had seemed receptive to his message suddenly burst into loud applause. On reflection he found there was a message here he did not want to face. For a second the silent majority had spoken and said quite simply, "Children are no damned good." Holt found he was having to come to terms with the evidence that suggested that most American adults actively distrust and dislike most children, even their own, and, quite often, especially their own.

Childhood is seen from this viewpoint as a period of reluctance to learn, incapability, avoidance of effort, of ignorance, and therefore unworthy of being granted any rights in law or in general consideration or indeed any respect. The most extreme version of this view holds that children are born evil. John Wesley had this to say about educating children:

"Break their wills betimes; begin this great work before they can run alone, before they can speak plain, or perhaps speak at all. Let him have nothing he cries for, absolutely nothing, great or small. Make him do as he is bid, if you whip him ten times running to effect it. Break his will now and his soul will live, and he will probably bless you to all eternity."

The theology may have faded or become humanised, but the message lingers on as this letter quoted somewhat approvingly in the Times Educational Supplement in 1984 suggests :

"So it's refreshing to discover a letter to the headmaster of Langley private school in Norwich from a father imploring the headmaster thus: 'You need to take James by the scruff of the neck, ram his nose into a book and kick his arse every time he gazes out of the window.'
The parent in question runs his own advertising and marketing agency. And marketing men have a way with words."

Husen (1974)in *The Learning Society* notes that the concept of school has been developed in the last hundred years or so on a number of assumptions held to be self-evident, yet all of them fallacious but plausible in action since they generate self-fulfilling prophecies. One refers to the learner as resister:

" Pupils undertake to learn mainly to avoid the disagreeable consequences if they do not : low marks, non-promotion, censure, punishment, etc."

The role of resister has to be learnt. The evidence from early childhood is that the problem is usually how to deal with the young child's exploration, desire to find out, and endless questions.

Learner as Receptacle

It is not easy to find explicit advocacy of the 'Jug and mugs' theory of education. Instead it appears to be accepted as the inevitable system. The jug-teacher possesses the knowledge thought to be essential and attempts to pour it into the rows of mug-learners empty and ready to be filled. It has historical associations with Locke's view of the learner as tabula rasa, the clean slate waiting for someone to write knowledge on to it. This apparently simple view of the role of the learner is the tip of an iceberg of assumptions. Rogers (1983) lists eight of them:
The teacher is the possessor of knowledge,the student the expected recipient.
Verbal instruction via lecture, textbook or formal lesson is the major means of transferring the knowledge from teacher to learner.

An examination measures the amount of transfer.
The teacher possesses power, the learner is the one who obeys.
Trust is at a minimum, in particular the teacher distrusts the learner.
Rule by authority and control by establishing an intermittent state of fear are the accepted classroom organisational policies.
Democracy and its values are ignored and scorned in practice.
There is no place for the whole person in education, only for her/his intellect.

Rogers is scathing in his criticism of this approach and proposes that teaching of the above kind is a relatively unimportant and overvalued activity because the only persons who are effectively educated in an environment that is constantly changing are the ones who have learned how to learn for themselves, who have learned to change and adapt, and who have realised that virtually no knowledge is secure.

Another writer uses an economic metaphor. The learners are like bank accounts into which deposits are regularly made. At times, these deposits are drawn on to cover requirements such as examinations, or essays, or even television quiz games. Freire (1972) describes this as the banking conception of education.

Learner as Raw Material

A variety of metaphors likens the learners to some form of raw material. In one view they are clay waiting to be moulded by the potter. In another they are like young trees or plants requiring the training and supporting skills of the gardener. Again, they can be seen as bricks requiring the skills of architect and builder to design and construct on sound foundations and principles. The learners are seen as in need of some enlightened manipulation so that they will fit into the slots in a relatively harmonious society. The learners are accorded no rights or even much say in the matter. Do potters consult with the clay, or gardeners with their plants or builders with their bricks? If this seems a little overstated, consider the research of Stone and Taylor (1976) who researched the legal cases involving pupils' rights. Their conclusion was that pupils had virtually no rights in law. In one example the courts found that pupils who were pacifists could still be compelled to join the cadet force of the school by a headteacher and the right of conscientious objection allowable to adults was overruled.

Learner as Client.

The education system can be seen to have multiple clients and they include parents, employers, and others such as product and service retailers who need pupils to become good consumers. The pupils themselves frequently come bottom of the list if they figure on it at all. Whenever committees or consultative bodies are set up to investigate and pronounce on some aspect of education, it is rare for the pupils to be represented.

The role of client implies some form of consultation and some use of the results as feedback. Attempts to research the pupils' viewpoint on schooling are not very common and often result in rather hysterical outbursts from adults. One headteacher responded to the idea of asking pupils' views on student teacher classroom performance with the assertion that it was dangerous to involve children in this kind of comment on their teachers and that the student who had volunteered to try this out was not to procede with the exercise. Another headteacher refused permission in another school stating that discipline would be adversely affected by this kind of exercise. A third expressed the judgment that such consultation would be bad for classroom relationships. Another asserted that children were not competent to judge these matters. These reactions occurred despite the fact that each headteacher had in front of them a written briefing showing the results of previous research studies in both the U.K. and U.S.A. and demonstrating that their judgments were not supported by the evidence and indeed that the facts were the opposite to what they believed. (see Meighan 1977).

The pupils on the other hand demonstrated high degrees of validity and reliability in their perceptions. The student teachers who were allowed to proceed reported improved relationships. The pupils frequently expressed the view that they felt confident in commenting on teaching performance since they were on the receiving end for hours and hours - at least 15,000 hours up to the age of sixteen.

Much has been made both by advocates and opponents, of the 'child-centred' nature of primary schooling in the U.K. This would imply that pupils in this age group at least were seen as clients. On closer examination little actual consultation can be traced and what is found instead is *child referencing* where adults define and deduce the needs and requirements from secondhand sources and then impose modified adult-selected and pre-planned material accordingly. Perhaps this just about qualifies as being seen as a client though it is rather limited in scope and not unlike the experience so many patients have with what is seen as the patronising style of their doctors.

Learner as Partner

Regarding the learner as partner denotes a shift of emphasis from consultation for feedback that the teacher might or might not act upon, to negotiation, where a right to be heard and to be considered is established. One family operating home-based education in this manner was the Harrison family. During a T.V. documentary in the B.B.C. Forty Minutes series, the father, Geoff Harrison, explained that in their approach, the youngest member of the family was seen as having equality of consideration and a right to be listened to so that his point of view could be taken into account. If a contribution from any member of the family was shown to be reasonable, then it would be included or accommodated in some way. It was the family's experience that sensible ideas and suggestions were to be gained from children and adults : the adults did not have a monopoly of wisdom or reason. The outcome was a negotiated curriculum and a cooperative approach to learning amongst partners. The partners may not be equal in all respects at a given time e.g. the adults may have more experience or information related to a particular learning activity. But such inequality was seen as temporary and could be reversed in situations where a child happened to have initial advantages in ideas or information. Freire (1972) describes this approach as that of the teacher' taking on the role of student amongst students'.

Learners would welcome this approach, Blishen (1969) concludes. In his book *The School That I'd Like*, Blishen analyses the essays of children writing about their experiences of school and how it might be improved. He notes the

"...children's longing to take upon themselves some of the burden of deciding what should be learnt, how it should be learnt: this desire to get closer to the raw matter of learning, not to be presented with pre-digested knowledge by teacher or textbook; above all to learn by talking, debating with the teacher as senior confederate rather than as sole provider. They want excitement; they want a form of learning for which the word , for so many of them, is 'research'; they want to discover how to be responsible for themselves and their own ideas."

The essays showed that there was a time for many learners when teachers did seem like partners and that was in their primary schools ; the step from primary to secondary frequently turned out to be a step from excitement and acceptance into boredom and rejection.

The research of Wells (1985) suggests that the quality may have been even higher for many before going to school if the learners could only remember that far back, since when children started school at five years of age, there was frequently a change in style from the sensitive and spontaneously constructive conversations with parents to the more limited exchanges with their infant teachers operating with more pre-set agendas, and of course larger numbers of learners and in some respects, more limiting conditions of work.

This relationship between learner and teacher has been expressed in other ways. It has been described as that of worker or co-worker in the review of school as organisations by Handy (1984). In the analysis of Rowland (1984 and 1988) the roles can become interchangeable to some extent as 'learners become teachers and teachers become learners' in an interactive and interpretative model of teaching and learning. Rowland (1988) concludes that :

"Such a model has been shown to provide a practical basis for teaching children in the classroom. It also offers a hope for a form of education in which learning takes place beyond the school-room and is integrated into our wider lives as we become teachers and learners for each other."

Learner as Autonomous Explorer.

In autonomous learning , the learner is a 'meaning maker' rather than a 'meaning receiver' to adopt the terminology of Postman and Weingartner (1971). The learners develop as researchers, master the logistics of learning how to learn and arrive at a point where they are capable of making all the decisions about what to study, the appropriate contents, methods and assessments. Since the emphasis is on study and research skills, the content on which these are developed and practised is less important a concern that in a transmission approach. In that approach it is held that the essential knowledge is not the skills of learning but a particular package of information offered in the form of what are claimed to be basic subjects. There is disagreement here as to what constitutes 'the basics' of education - memorised information or learning skills.

The two ideas are not mutually exclusive. Teachers can employ individualised work approaches which carry a hidden curriculum of study methods. These methods hold their own or are even superior in transmission terms since blocks of information are effectively learnt and can be repeated in examinations if required, but they have the bonus of developing research and study skills in the process. The most developed example is perhaps that of the Open University which replaces the mass lecture with study units for use at home. Such individualised systems can deliberately use one as a prelude to the other by starting with a teaching system that utilises autonomous study purely for transmission purposes and then gradually allowing the learner access to more and more of the decision making, graduating to a 'How To Make Your Own Study Unit'. The Open University has not got this far and learners remain dependant on course unit writers, and so are only partially autonomous.

In early childhood education, the High Scope approach developed by Wiekart in the U.S.A. takes autonomous learning as the top priority. The formula for young learners is 'plan, do, review' and the teachers implement this approach from the outset. The learners are seen as autonomous explorers of their environment using the available adults as guides. This also tends to be the major approach adopted sooner or later in families that decide to educate their children at home.

Learner as Democratic Explorer

In autonomous learning, the learner becomes personally responsible and develops individually. Democratic learning implies a group working in cooperation where the group of learners devise their own programme, implement it and evaluate it, using the teachers as resources as the group sees appropriate. Adapting the Wiekart formula, the group 'plans, does and reviews.'

The democratic approach can exist in varying degrees. In a syndicate approach, learners work to a pre-set syllabus or content but the methods of learning are left to the group to decide. A project approach allows democratic learning for a specific part of a course only. A learning cooperative makes all decisions about course content, methods and resources but has to meet externally imposed assessment requirements in some way.

The approaches of autonomous learning and democratic learning can be seen as complementary to some extent. The research required for effective group sessions is done by individuals or pairs or small working parties where the skills of autonomous study are very useful. Autonomous learning sooner or later requires some contact of a cooperative nature with groups, organisations or institutions for access to experiences or information.

Democratic learning generates a variety of consequences. Some sense of community is likely to develop within the group. A working partnership develops with the appointed teachers. These appointed teachers need to have trust in the ability and creative power of their fellow humans who come to them in the role of student. Dialogue becomes a major activity rather than formal instruction. The specimen contract given below indicates some of the features of democratic learning:

Group Learning Contract

We agree to accept responsibility for our course as a group.

We agree to take an active part in the learning of the group.

We agree to be constructively critical of our own and other people's ideas.

We agree to plan our own programme of studies, implement it using the group members and appointed teachers as resources, and review the outcomes in order that we may learn from any limitations we identify.

We agree to the keeping of a group log-book of work completed, planning decisions, session papers and any other appropriate documents.

We agree to share the duties of being in the chair, the task of being meeting secretary and the roles of session organisers and contributors.

We agree to review this contract from time to time.

Conclusion.

There is no generally agreed categorisation of learning roles. The seven listed above do not exhaust all the possibilities but they serve to demonstrate that a variety exists. Some of the alternatives are more rigid and others more flexible. It is not the point of flexischooling necessarily to exclude any, but to move from situations that do practise exclusion, to ones that do not. The more flexible role definitions, however, do tend to include many of the others, so that a group of learners working in a democratic mode may make use of or deal with most of the role definitions in its programme of studies. The reverse is not the case, however : e.g. where learning situations are set up on the theory that learners are resisters, other possibilities are unlikely to develop. A common illustration of this is the situation where teachers complain that their senior pupils will not take the opportunity now offered to them to engage in dialogue and discussion. After years of becoming trained and habituated to the one role on offer - that of passive receiver, the learners are suddenly expected to exhibit new habits. Ironically and unjustly, they are then blamed in terms of their personal inadequacy as people when they do not instantly reverse their behaviour. More to the point would be to identify the rigidity of the learning regime they have been subjected to as the culprit.

Chapter Four

The Teachers : A Repertoire of Roles

"Teaching is more difficult than learning because what teaching calls for is this : to let learn"
                                        Martin Heidegger in *What is Called Thinking?*

It comes as something of a surprise that there is still no agreed classification of teaching and the role of teachers. In the literature there are numerous attempts to contrast two pairs of teaching styles but as I have demonstrated elsewhere, these are selections from a larger agenda of possibilities.(see Meighan 1986)

In the absence of anything more appropriate, I shall base the analysis here on the classification into a group of authoritarian and a group of non-authoritarian roles. The latter divides into two sub-groups of autonomous approaches and democratic approaches which can be seen as interactive and interdependent rather than necessarily in rivalry, as I hope to show.

Authoritarian Teaching Roles

The forms or sub-types of authoritarian teaching may vary but the basic assumption is constant. It is that one person (the teacher) is dominant and the other or others is or are dependent. The teacher decides, the learner or learners are required to respond. This is true of all aspects of the relationship : the control aspects of the situation are seen as the responsibility of the teacher, so is the selection of contents of what is to be learnt and so are the chosen modes or methods of attempted learning and its assessment.

Although power lies firmly in the hands of the teacher in authoritarian approaches, the form that this takes varies and one source of variation is where some delegation of decision making is granted to the learners. The most restricted and least flexible form is the autocratic.

(a) *Autocratic.*
In the autocratic form, order is obtained through the use of fear which may be physical or psychological or both. The images associated are those of a ringmaster, a commanding officer or a dictator and the style is openly cooercive. Advocates of this approach speak enthusiastically about 'firm discipline' for the learners are frequently perceived as resisters. (The learners ,on the other hand, have been known to describe such teachers as constipated people.)

(b) *Parental*
Order is obtained through deference in the parental form where the related images are those of persuasive mother, father, priest or village policeman. The description of 'benign dictatorship' is sometimes applied. The maternal variant is commonly

observed in primary schools and the paternal variant commonly seen in secondary schools. Learners are usually seen as receptacles or as raw material.

(c) *Charismatic.*
In this form, order is obtained through personal charm, public performance skills and good-humoured repartee. The images associated with this approach are those of a leader with disciples, an entertainer with fans or a pied piper with followers. Learners are perceived as audience or as followers. Secondary school teachers who can achieve this style enjoy high levels of popularity with their students.

(d) *The Expert*
In playing the expert variant of authoritarian control, the stress is on the information possessed by the teacher which the learners are induced to believe is necessary, or useful or special. Related images are those of the sage, or doctor, scientist or medicine man and a more specific form of deference is invoked than in the parental form.. Teachers of examination groups may often use this approach, and science teachers in secondary schools often have an elaborate set design of benches, unfamiliar equipment and fittings which can support such a role interpretation. The learners tend to be seen as receptacles.

(e) *Organisational*
The organisational form of authoritarian control can be one of the most deceptive. Order is obtained through detailed organisation, indicating a clear structure, operated through precise instructions to ends and means planned in a systematic way. The images associated are those of an architect, a production planner or television script writer. Students may appear to be behaving independently, working on individual assignments it would seem and indeed some decisions may have been delegated to them, but in all key respects, the teacher has planned and continues to control the system. Learners are perceived as raw material. In higher education, the Open University system operates in this way.

(f) *Consultative*
In consultative forms of order, feedback from the learners is used to establish and to modify the learning programmes. The role of student is more interactive in that the teacher has taken some account of the ideas and responses of the group members. The teacher, however, retains the veto throughout and remains in overall control. Learners tend to be seen more in the role of clients.

In all these forms of control, the dominance of the teacher persists and the dependence of the learner remains unless the teacher decides otherwise. But the degree of dependence varies from type to type so that with the autocratic it is often 100% but with the consultative it can be much lower. Putting it another way, these styles vary in their flexibility.

Flexischooling would imply that teachers would seek the most flexible form of teaching that a situation will sustain and would see the more rigid forms as only temporary expedients. This is in contrast to the orthodox view that there is a right way to teach which needs to be identified and then implemented on a permanent basis. Some teachers are part of the way towards this practice in that they use a combination of the sub-types outlined above, often changing style with the age of the learners. In the case of secondary school teachers, they may well approach seventeen year old pupils in a less rigid way than eleven year olds. But there may be no recognition that in their primary schools the learners may have been used to more flexible approaches anyway, so that the style encountered on transfer may represent a regression..

Non-Authoritarian Teaching Roles

The repertoire of teaching styles from which a teacher can select stretches beyond the authoritarian grouping. Non-authoritarian teaching roles may be seen as falling into two groups, autonomous and democratic. In both cases there is a shift towards power sharing.

(a) *Autonomous Study and the Teacher's Role*
This approach signifies that the teacher negotiates most if not all of the features of the study programme and that a learner has some degree of power and responsibility for the learning from the start. That power and responsibility can then be increased over time. A variety of terms have been used to identify this approach, including individualised learning, personalised instruction, independent learning, and self-directed learning. These terms can be used to indicate a shift of emphasis since 'individualised learning' suggests that the system is set up by a teacher for a learner and at this stage is authoritarian somewhat in the organisational mode outlined above. But 'self-directed learning' suggests that a learner has gradually moved on from this starting point, acquired more and more of the decision-making skills, and experienced a transfer of power. At some point the learner has reduced dependence on the teacher to a stage where they can be regarded as more autonomous than dependent. The move has taken place from an authoritarian situation to a non-authoritarian. The learner has become autonomous explorer.

The activity of the teacher is complex and requires the skills of providing advice, of facilitating the learning, of learning alongside the student if the content is new or unfamiliar, and of assisting with appropriate assessments. In providing for the accumulation of decision making and study skills with the accompanying and gradual transfer of power, teachers are deliberately making themselves redundant for this particular learner. The provision of a Resources Bank or even a school or college Resources Centre can result from the widespread adoption of this approach to learning and teaching. Autonomous learners gradually become competent enough to contribute some of their work to the collection for use by others (see Taylor 1971).

(b) *Democratic Learning and the Role of the Teacher*

If autonomous study is somewhat rare in the U.K. system, democratic learning is even rarer. In democratic learning the group of learners take on substantial degrees of decision making. The group devises and implements its own programme of studies to some extent or other. As we saw in the previous chapter, the democratic approach can exist in various forms and the role of the teacher varies somewhat with each.

(i) Project Approach

A project approach allows democratic learning for a specific part of a course only. Although the teachers retain overall control of the syllabus and the learning programme they decide that for one part of the work to delegate power. Learners are given the chance to choose a topic, investigate it together, produce and present findings which may then be subject to assessment. (If this is organised by teachers as individual rather than group projects, then it falls into the repertoire of autonomous possibilities.) The role of the teacher is somewhat inconsistent, requiring a sudden switch into advising and facilitating, often somewhat startling learners who are used to teacher as instructor.

(ii) Syndicate Approach

In this approach, the syllabus or content is set by the teachers or examination board but the methods of learning along with the resources are delegated by the teacher to the learning group who debate and select the most effective way of learning for their situation to achieve the pre-set goals. The role of the teacher is composite with authoritarian monitoring of content and syllabus coverage alternating with the necessary facilitation and servicing of the remaining democratic activity.

(iii) Learning Cooperative

Learning cooperatives make all the decisions about course content, methods of learning and the selection of appropriate resources. Their syllabus is a blank piece of paper. They have to meet some externally imposed form of assessment, although this may often be flexible enough to be only a minimum constraint. The role of the teacher shows more consistency here in requiring the facilitation of the decisions of the group and contributing advice - a kind of civil servant model of helping implement the group's policy making.

(iv) Independent Learning Cooperative

In the rarest situation of all, the group is entirely democratic and takes all decisions including those of appropriate assessment. The University of the Third Age appears to operate in this way with completely independent self-programming groups.

Conclusion

There may be other ways of classifying teaching roles but the one adopted above demonstrates that there is a repertoire of possibilities. A more flexible approach could begin with operating just within the full range of authoritarian possibilities and the gains of this should not be discounted. The extension into the consultative form would in itself be a considerable act of flexibility in some situations.

The movement into non-authoritarian teaching roles is something of a journey into uncharted waters and there is only limited research and reportage to offer guidance. One issue is that of the relationship between the two groups of autonomous and democratic approaches. Do we have to choose between autonomy or democracy? The answer lies in demonstrating how they can be complementary and interactive. Effective democracy requires some of the skills of autonomy in its members as individuals pool their knowledge, experience and ideas for mutual benefit. Otherwise they pool merely their ignorance. Autonomy divorced from democracy excludes learners from group co-operative experiences : purely autonomous learners exclude themselves from experiences such as membership of orchestras, drama groups and learning co-operatives and are destined to become educational hermits.

It is sometimes fashionable to decry authoritarian teaching roles altogether but the proposal in respect of the concept of flexischooling is that they have a legitimate place. The proviso is that they are seen as temporary expedients rather than the Final Solution, as part of the means to the end and not mistaken for the end itself. The analogy of a rocket launch in space research may be indicative: authoritarian teaching roles may be part of the first stage of the launch, but they are destined to fall away to leave the rocket to continue its voyage of discovery. They also have a place when a group of learners choose to submit themselves to authoritarian learning because they define this as the most effective way for them to learn a particular thing.

The current profile of teaching roles is erratic. In early childhood education in the U.K., children are likely to experience some forms of autonomous learning within an authoritarian general setting, which gives way to more emphasis on authoritarian teaching styles as they approach secondary schooling. At secondary schooling they are likely to experience an increase in the more rigid forms of teaching. Those who survive into further education may begin to experience some autonomous learning again. Democratic learning is usually conspicuous by its absence from this profile. The results of this kind of profile have been variously and scathing described as *Compulsory Mis-education* (Goodman 1971) and *The Betrayal of Youth* (Hemming 1980) The proposal of flexischooling is to work for a less erratic profile which includes the whole repertoire of possibilities and moves from the more rigid to the more flexible forms of teaching and learning experiences.

Chapter Five

Flexibility and the Curriculum

"If a curriculum is to be effective in the classroom it must contain different ways of activating children, different ways of presenting sequences, different opportunities for some children to 'skip' parts while others work their way through different ways of putting things. A curriculum in short, must contain many tracks leading to the same general goal."

Jerome Bruner in *The Process of Education*

Curriculum Alternatives

Attempts to define the curriculum vary. Some concentrate on the idea of what is deliberately instructional and limit attention to what appears on timetables. An extension of this approach is to include other learning experiences provided they are intentional and therefore extra-curricular activities such as school clubs and societies are seen as part of the curriculum. A wider definition includes anything that is learnt in school and therefore includes a hidden curriculum of other things that are learnt in addition to the official curriculum as well as some often unintentional messages from the instructional activity itself.

Another approach has been to define what is excluded on the grounds that a curriculum refers to what learners are given the opportunity to learn and that this implies a null curriculum of what is denied, whether intentionally or not.

A curriculum thus becomes a study of what is valued and given priority in preference to what is denied and devalued. Thus Drill used to be part of the U.K. curriculum but it gave way to Physical Education. An ancient language Latin is still available to some, although it has lost its former central position, whereas the international language of Esperanto is largely excluded.

There is a variety of attempts to classify alternative ideas about the curriculum and listing these should demonstrate that we are dealing with a complex concept:

> Open v. Closed
> Teacher centred v. Child centred
> National v. Professional
> Sexist v. Non-sexist
> Racist v. Non-racist
> Confidence building v. Confidence destructive
> Past oriented v. Future oriented
> Thought control v Freethought
> Ageist v. Lifelong
> Subject v. Lifeskills
> Authoritarian v. Non-authoritarian
> Regimental v. Diversified

The debates about curriculum have tended to attempt to decide for or against one or other of these sets of ideas. The argument of this chapter is that a more flexible approach to the curriculum can include quite a few of the above possibilities, though not all.

The most rigid forms of curriculum tend to those that are imposed on learners with a view to controlling their thought. In religious versions the excluded ideas are labelled heresy. In a National Curriculum the heresy is more likely to be political.

Six different types of curriculum are discussed in this chapter. They are :

- the imposed subjects
- the imposed interpretative
- the imposed confidence-building
- the consultative
- the negotiated
- the democratic

The Imposed Subjects Curriculum

Compulsory schooling has relied heavily on the idea that someone or some persons know what is best for other people to know, think and do. It has relied on there being a willingness to force all others to accept their conclusions. This idea might have more plausibility if there were agreement about what is worth knowing. Consider, though, the religious versions of imposed curricula. The the rival versions of Christianity have never shown consensus. In particular, they have shown disagreement as to whether the key authority was the Church, The Bible, in one of its rival versions, or the Inner Light. Across religions, the disagreements multiply and the Islamic curriculum of Iran would hardly meet with approval in Judiac circles, or Hindu, or Buddhist.

The secular option of a National Curriculum might seem likely to generate more consensus but in practice this is not the case. The selection of subjects, their content, and the amount of time to be devoted to each varies from case to case. Bertrand Russell noted the problem when writing in 1916 :

"It is in history and religion and other controversial subjects that the actual instruction is positively harmful. These subjects touch the interests by which the schools are maintained; and the interests maintain the schools in order that certain views on these subjects may be instilled. History, in every country, is so taught as to magnify that country: children learn to believe that their own country has always been in the right and almost always victorious, and that it has produced almost all the great men, and that it is in all respects superior to all other countries. Since these beliefs are flattering, they are easily absorbed and hardly ever dislodged from instinct by later knowledge."

Passing over a somewhat odd use of the word instinct here, and noting that recent work of the hidden curriculum suggests that all subjects including the supposedly abstract Mathematics carry political messages, Russell is proposing that religious bigotry is replaced by political bigotry, merely an alternative form of thought control.. To what extent is this accurate?

The National Curriculum of the USSR has as its central aim the production of young communists with subjects and contents chosen accordingly, whereas the aim in Hitler's Germany was to produce young fascists and required a different set of contents. Sweden has a National Curriculum with a different purpose, to produce young people committed to active involvement in democratic institutions underpinned by the concept of welfare capitalism. In this cause 17% of the curriculum is devoted to the social sciences. The U.K. National Curriculum excludes the social sciences from the required curriculum altogether on the charge that they provoke children to critical thought. (Teachers of these subjects in the U.K. on the other hand report that the outcome of their teaching is largely that of fatalism rather than reforming zeal.)

Imposed curricula frequently represent a kind of ancestor worship in their reliance on subjects as the principal component. The subject divisions devised by our ancestors are held to be basically sound. It is not too difficult to demonstrate that this is dubious and that the current issues that are of central concern are cross disciplinary if not super-disciplinary. Concerns such as the Mass Media, Pollution, Modern Terrorism, Space Research and Computer Technology were not part of the societies that devised the division into subjects.

The Imposed Interpretative Curriculum

The interpretative curriculum is based on similar assumptions to the imposed subjects curriculum in that it is assumed that adults know best what it is children should ultimately learn and know. There is, however, a different view as to how this might be achieved. In this approach, some active involvement of the learners is attempted by encouraging a dialogue between the learner's existing stock of knowledge and those of the teacher. The most developed version of this view is found in U.K. primary schools and in particular, in early childhood education. In attempting such a dialogue, a much looser and more flexible view of knowledge is seen as appropriate, often more present-orientated in the selection of topics.. The framework is seen as Language, Mathematics, Art, Drama, Music, Physical Education, Science Studies, etc., often learnt through exploring inter-connected themes, as the basis for more subject focused work later. The task of the teacher is seen as starting with the consciousness of the learner and interpreting this in terms of the knowledge valued by the school and its teachers.

This approach has somewhat erroneously been called child-centred. A more appropriate description might be *child-referenced* in that adults make some reference to the world of the children in order to move them into knowledge the adults regard as desirable. The child-centred approach is more commonly found in the work of parents with their children up to the age of five as the research of Wells indicated. The achievement of spoken language is the result of a such a child-centred regime with parents responding to the spontaneous interests of their child rather than working to any attempted systematic scheme of events. The contrast can be made with how teachers try to teach a second language using systematic and at the most, a child-referenced approach, with usually much poorer results than the parents achieved with the first language.

This alternative approach to an imposed curriculum suffers from similar problems to the imposed subjects curriculum in that there is no consensus about what is worth knowing. Some children may find the topic of dinosaurs appearing for the third time in their primary school careers yet no attention at all given to other themes such as environmental pollution. Where, as so often is the case, Social and Political themes are missing from the agenda, the children are left to the mercies of comics, tabloid newspapers and television to fill the gaps. A National Curriculum provides no answer to this problem as we saw above because it turns out to be just another arbitrary adult-centered selection of knowledge reflecting the values or 'hang-ups' of the minority of adults who made the selection.

Imposed Confidence-Building Curriculum

The approach through future-orientated views of knowledge is to give top priority to the skills of learning themselves since they are seen as permanent in contrast to specific blocks of information which are seen as liable to become dated or redundant. In this approach to the curriculum the confidence to learn and re-learn and the skills of finding or creating information, organising, sifting and evaluating findings can be practised on a variety of topics so that the need for a set agenda is avoided. Fragmentation is not seen as a critical problem since the learners are acquiring the tools to fill gaps as and when necessary. The approach is seen as self-correcting in this respect.

The learners are still working to the formulas of adults but to a different set of formulas from those of the subjects school of thought or from those of the interpretation methods and integrated topics persuasion. This approach does imply more flexibility than the previous two versions of the imposed curriculum, as Hemming (1984) notes in his proposals for a confidence-building curriculum :

"Confidence grows from the use of personal powers. But children vary infinitely in their capacities and interests. It follows that the school must present wide variety in its curriculum, as well as assuring the acquisition of basic skills - the tools for dealing with the world. Only by offering a range of stimuli,in school and out, can we provide appropriate nourishment for personal growth. We cannot tell what stimulus will be a source of growth for any individual child. Hence we should not set out with too many pre-conceived ideas about what growing points we should seek to implant in the child's mind. Since we now know that everything

interrelates with everything else......any point of entry that stirs interest, and is pursued with fascination, ultimately can bring a child into contact with the whole spectrum of human knowledge."

In contrast to John Wesley's view quoted earlier that the child's will must be broken at all costs to achieve obedience, Hemming proposes that the breaking of youthful confidence is desperately damaging to both the individual and to society: the cost of trying to control or rehabilitate the mis-educated, anti-social and resentful members of society runs into billions of pounds a year, he argues, and represents an enormous amount of personal misery.

The Consultative Curriculum.

A consultative curriculum is initially based on an imposed programme. This may be one of the three types outlined above or some combination of them since they do not necessarily exist in isolation. Into this imposed curriculum is built regular opportunities for the learners to be consulted about the programme. Their feedback is then reflected upon by the teacher and modifications to the curriculum may then be sanctioned. Although the learners now have the opportunity to have their say, the veto is firmly retained by the teacher who decides whether the feedback can be incorporated into the existing scheme of things.

The idea of consulting with learners is often viewed with suspicion and sometimes hostility in spite of the evidence that pupils rarely make more than modest and sober suggestions when involved in such exercises. Indeed the radical view that learners are a reservoir of untapped desires and yearning to take charge of their learning, their curriculum and their schools, does not square with the evidence available. Their 'demands' turn out to be a somewhat wistful desire for a more kindly and considerate authoritarian regime than the one they are used to. Blishen (1969) in his book *The School That I'd Like* based on the essays of pupils in U.K. schools noted that

"....the evidence of all this writing is that our children are immensely anxious to be reasonable, to take account of practical difficulties."

The same is true of my own researches into the pupil perspective in the 1970's and of recent studies since then. (e.g. White and Brockington 1983.) Elements of the consultative curriculum can be found in many primary schools and it is this kind of experience that the pupils in Blishen's sample rated highly :

"For many of them, there was a time when learning was discovery, and teachers seemed to be older partners, and that was in the primary school. There are children's words quoted in this book that glow with the memory of good primary school teaching, when you were fully involved - head, heart, imagination. It is a miserable thing that the step taken by so many of our children when they pass to the secondary school, should be a step from excitement and acceptance into boredom and rejection."

In a more recent exercise in 1984, The Northamptonshire Local Education Authority organised a series of one day conferences for secondary pupils to elicit their views about the curriculum before the officers replied to the Department of Education and Science policy statement *A Framework for the Curriculum*. The account by Makins (1984) outlines the reservations of the pupils and notes the rather modest suggestions for reform. These included a request that pupils be given more opportunities for participation in the running of the schools and consulted regularly about the curriculum. The existing curriculum was seen as giving too much emphasis to the academic tradition and not enough attention to current day issues and needs.

The curriculum in Sweden is National and Imposed for the majority of the time but the minority time curriculum is left for optional studies. Some of these are courses offered by the teachers and some are courses based on ideas obtained from the pupils by consultation, which the school then facilitates. Given that this operates in a school organisational structure that insists on pupil unions being available, and provides for the democratic involvement of the learners in the general running of the schools, I found Swedish pupils tended to be more satisfied with their learning opportunities than the U.K. pupils I have researched.

The Negotiated Curriculum.

In the negotiated curriculum, the degree of power sharing increases. The teacher is in the role of persuader, and uses reason rather than the veto. What emerges is an agreed contract with individuals and sometimes groups as to the nature of the course of study to be undertaken. The negotiation constitutes an attempt to link the concerns and consciousness of the learners with the world of systematic knowledge and learning. This can take several forms.

In The City As School, a High school in New York, the negotiation is about which work experience and its associated learning programme the learner would like next. They may have completed one chosen assignment attached to a printing firm and now elect to experience the world of the journalist attached to a newspaper office. The curriculum consists of regular negotiations of this kind using a prospectus of opportunities which is constantly being expanded and revised using, amongst other things, learner ideas and feedback.

Some schools in the U.K. have introduced more flexibility in their curriculum by suspending the timetable for short periods of time. Sometimes this has been for one day a term, in other cases one day a month. One school, Stantonbury Campus, has instituted a Day Ten when every tenth day is used in this way, and another, Sutton Centre allocates two weeks a year, one in December and one in July. The programme of activities for these periods of time is negotiated amongst staff and pupils.

The approach through a negotiated curriculum was widely adopted in the U.K. in the Youth Training Schemes set up by the Manpower Services Commission. Here school leavers joining the ranks of the four million or so unemployed at the time, were involved in training schemes where it was seen that to repeat the imposed forms of curricula that these young people had already experienced in schools with scant success, was inappropriate. Instead, programmes were negotiated between staff and learners within the resources and guidelines available.

One curriculum with considerable experience of a negotiated approach is that of the Duke of Edinburgh's Award Scheme. Substantial parts of the award programme are negotiated with the learner who chooses activities from the menu on offer.

The Democratic Curriculum

When a group of learners write, implement and review their own curriculum starting out with a blank piece of paper, power sharing has reached the point of democratic practice. The learners take on the roles of researchers and explorers and the teachers take on the roles of facilitators and fixers. The writer's own experience of this approach has been in teacher training and in in-service courses with experienced teachers.(Meighan and Harber 1987) Since 1976, the teachers in training concerned have been given the opportunity to choose their learning approach. On offer was an imposed curriculum, a negotiated alternative or a democratic option. The course thus begins in a consultative mode as the tutor takes the initiative to outline the possibilities and then in most cases has switched to a democratic mode as the group has decided to design, teach and evaluate its own course and to operate as a learning co-operative. Each course has written an evaluation of the experience and these accounts contain many comments of which these are typical :

"The co-operative spent many hours in discussion and formulated opinions and views (often varying) in relation to our timetable of work. All the group members felt without any reservation whatsoever that the co-op was a new working experience which was stimulating, enjoyable and very worthwhile. We all gained an enormous amount from it academically and in relation to the new relationships we formed."

"Democratic responsibility, as opposed to sitting back and always receiving, meant that the students had to use the skills they already had, as well as learning new ones. Such a situation was a good one in which to develop confidence in one's own thinking."

Conclusion.

The classification of the curriculum offered above is not the only one available nor does it exhaust the possibilities, thus no mention has been made of the idea of a largely spontaneous curriculum with emergent networked structures rather than those pre-planned and imposed. Here a programme develops in the form of episodes, spontaneous modules or projects rather than courses, with the learner or learners acting autonomously. Such a curriculum has been adopted by some families in their home-based educational alternative to schools and in particular, though not exclusively, by families operating an alternative life-style based on self-sufficiency.

Some families operate a flexible curriculum in terms of including several of the above types in their programme. Often the morning programme may be imposed and pre-planned, sometimes to satisfy the wishes of the Local Education Officers, sometimes for external examination purposes, and sometimes for reasons of the family's own. The afternoon programme may then be of another kind, consultative, negotiated, or democratic in cooperation with another family. These families have pointed the way to how flexischooling can work in terms of a more flexible approach to the curriculum by operating with several types rather than limiting themselves to one approach, and also in terms of moving on from the more rigid imposed forms to the more learner-involving variants over time.

An essential part of the approach of the families working in these flexible ways is the regular monitoring and evaluation of their curriculum. In some cases I have seen this taking place regularly and deliberately at morning coffee breaks supplemented by reviews at meal times. In other cases the planning and review has taken place in a regular Sunday evening meeting to decide the learning programme in outline for the following week. Informal contracts emerge on such occasions which could be more formally devised in the cases of schools working in this way and similar to the contracts that are found in the cases of Further Education Colleges that operate Flexistudy programmes with individual students.

Chapter Six.

Resources, Locations and Contracts : Schools as Learning Resource Centres.

" They know enough who know how to learn."

Henry Adams in *Education of Henry Adams*

Other Dimensions

The apparently simple notion that we explore the consequences of a more flexible approach to education has revealed a repertoire of possibilities in several dimensions : the role of the parents, the role of the learners, the role of the teachers and the forms of the curriculum. A number of dimensions remain to be explored and these include :
>the resources for learning
>the locations for learning
>the varieties of assessment
>the agendas of aims
>alternative forms of organisation

The Resources for Learning.

When mass schooling was established in the 1870's, the effective choice of the basic resources for learning was between teachers and books. When Charlotte Mason began teaching in 1861 she favoured the latter declaring that too much faith was commonly placed in oral lessons since they gave the child the minimum of mental labour. Formal instructional lessons should be few and far between and the majority of the time spent on books, supplemented by other activities such as nature study and the study of paintings. With her interest in home-based education, she did not assume that the organisation of this regular exposure to books and the establishment of the essential study habits that were required, necessitated a trained teacher. A parent following the method she devised would be equally effective and thus the Parent's National Educational Union was born along with the courses that have stood the test of a hundred years of use, revision and development. They are still widely used throughout the world and available through the World-wide Education Service based in London.

Today, the situation is radically changed because of the arrival on the scene of radio, television, film and the development of other forms of mass communication. People, as we noted in an earlier chapter, are surrounded by educative resources readily available and now augmented by personal computers, teletext, and video tapes. This situation has been described as that of *The Learning Society (*Husen 1974 and

1979) an expression that assumes that the salient features of the learning environment are those of change : a rapidly changing technology and a changing material and social world. As Husen notes, the requirements for a member of a static and conservative society can be acquired before entry to adulthood and the individual is supposed to draw substantially on that deposit of young learning for the rest of their life. In a time of relentless change, however, predicting the specific competencies needed a few decades or even a few years ahead becomes increasing difficult, prone to error and hazardous and gives way to notions of learning, re-learning and unlearning redundant ways, information and ideas.

"The implication for formal schooling is that its emphasis should be on skills and concepts that are applicable to a broad and largely unforeseen range of situations." (Husen 1979)

Resources for learning can be categorised in a variety of ways. They may be contrasted in terms of first-hand, second-hand or third-hand experiences. In the case of first-hand experiences the learners do the research, make the textbook or reading book, compile the dossiers of information, take part in a simulation perhaps of their own devising, make a tape slide, a television programme or mount an exhibition. In second-hand experiences they engage with the reported first-hand experiences of others given in books, films, television or by visiting speaker or in a teacher's formal lesson. In third-hand experiences summaries and digests of what people other than the writer or speaker experienced or thought are made available to learners in textbooks, lectures, news broadcasts or some other format.

Resources may be assembled in different orders of priorities. If books written by others are seen as the prime resource the school is likely to develop libraries: a school library, class libraries, and subject department collections in storerooms. If multi-media materials are seen as the prime resource then school resource centres may be the outcome and books somewhat dethroned to that of one useful resource amongst many. If first-hand experiences are elevated to the status of prime resource then the whole environment of the learners in school, at home and in the community is made available. In the U.K. the activity known as work-experience has gradually become adopted by increasing numbers of secondary schools in line with this approach. The idea was adopted much earlier in Sweden and the first work-experience for pupils there can now occur in the equivalent of their primary schools as the first of several such experiences. In the U.S.A. the school known as City As School in New York takes up this idea as the core element in its curriculum and organises learning around a series of prolonged work placements. The Parkway Programme in Philadelphia operates as a school without special buildings basing its courses and learning experiences in locations in the community.

Another way of classifying resources is in terms of access. Resources may be available to learners in varying degrees and in the most limited form available only through a teacher who has the storeroom key or is assumed to have precious subject knowledge. Resources may be limited for the most part to one sex as in the cases of Home Economics courses. The school resource centre may be freely available only to teachers or senior pupils. Resources may be restricted to insiders only and community schools have been at pains to operate on the different assumption that both insiders and outsiders should have some access. Open access to all is another possibility and Public Libraries and Museums already operate this way for their services.

As in the cases of the other aspects of education reviewed, the point of exploring the consequences of a more flexible policy is not to stigmatise any of these ideas about resources as automatically good or bad but to consider the possibility of regarding them as a complete repertoire of possibilities that can all be found some place at some stage in a flexischooling approach.

The Locations for Learning

One of the most taken-for-granted aspects of education has been location in a special building i.e. a school. Advocates of mass schooling in the 1870's had a simple answer to the problem of where to base education : if it made sense to move industrial activity from home situations and cottage industries to factories, the same thinking could be applied to education and move it away from homes into schools. As we saw, Charlotte Mason was more flexible in her thinking and saw both home-based education and school-based education as feasible, and in case parents did not wish to organise education at home themselves, trained home tutors/governesses and schoolteachers side by side following similar courses of study in the college at Ambleside. The same thinking applied to higher education : a university or college building was seen as essential. Correspondence courses using home as the base became regarded as rather second class substitutes for the 'real thing' and undertaken somewhat furtively. The establishment of the Open University in the 1970's using the technological resources available at home, i.e. radio, television, tape-recorders, kitchens for science experimental kits, the telephone and the postal service, shattered the orthodoxy. The establishment of Education Otherwise as the self-help group for parents electing to educate their children at home rather than use schools occurred soon afterwards in 1976-7. The events were not entirely unconnected since some of the parents involved were following Open University courses themselves and finding the experience exhilarating, so that when their children lost out in institutionalised learning the idea of a home-based alternative had plausibilty.

Other ideas were serving to challenge the orthodoxy of education limited to a school building. One was that of work experience and links with industry where the awareness developed that school had somehow become almost completely insulated from the major activity of the adult population. The tentative Understanding Industrial Society initiative of two Warwickshire Local Authority staff members in the 1960's, Alan Sanday and Peter Birch, failed to impress the funding committees of the Schools Council. A few years later two heavily funded projects were established to reinvent the wheel the Warwickshire based project had pioneered. Locating some activity in work places gradually became commonplace in the form of work experience.

Another initiative was that of the complex and ambiguous set of ideas which became known as the Community Schools movement. With at least ninety- four definitions of community as counted by Hillery (1955), debate about Community Schools always seems to begin, and ultimately founder and splinter on defining what the term means. In most of the rival versions of Community Schools, however, a more flexible set of locations is envisaged with the buildings and resources of the local community being regarded as part of the educational repertoire, as well as the school buildings being open to adult members as well as their children.

As mentioned earlier, the Parkway Programme in Philadelphia and the City As School initiatives in the U.S.A. not only expanded the concept of resources for learning, but also questioned the orthodoxy of a special building called a school as being sufficient for effective education to take place. The thinking is similar to that of the so-called deschooling writers who had a view of learning in a complex industrial and post-industrial as being located almost anywhere and their list of locations was extensive : libraries, museums, farms, streets, concert halls, homes, cinemas, factories, shops, offices, parks, and also schools redesigned as 'learning resource centres' rather than 'day detention centres'.

The Varieties of Assessment

Assessment is a regular feature of everyday life in that we all continually collect information about people, products, places, holiday possibilities, on the dress, behaviour and values of others, on television, news, consumer goods, and sport, to name but a few, and then pass judgment upon them. In education this activity is rife both at informal levels as pupils assess teachers , pupils assess fellow pupils, teachers observe and judge both pupils and fellow teachers as well as the parents who come their way. A small amount of this incessant assessment activity is selected out for more formal attention in the guise of marks, grades, tests and certificates. The formal assessment has been seen as carrying a somewhat complex and insidious set of messages that the participants learn in a process analogous to learning a board game like Monopoly where the operating rules are picked up as you go along without any opportunity or encouragement to question the assumptions, the information, the evidence or to debate whether there are better games that might be occupying the time. In the last resort, however, you can refuse to play Monopoly as an unworthy use of time if you so decide, unlike school assessment which turns out to be compulsory.

In the assessment activities as found in schools and other educational institutions, there exists a large repertoire of possibilities. The view of who is the appropriate person to assess ranges from the notion that it is a paid external examiner of an expensive-to-run examination board, through that of the teachers in day-to-day contact with the learners, to that of the learners themselves. There is a variety of proposals as to what should be assessed ranging from the courses, as to their efficiency in teaching the learners, to the teachers, as to their efficacy as educators, to the pupils, for their performance and achievement in learning. The purposes of assessment present a similar range of alternatives including a diagnostic intention to cure faulty learning, a developmental intention to indicate the next direction of learning, and a selective intention to sort learners into categories for differential treatment, e.g. as 'suitable' or 'not suitable' for further educational opportunities at a university.

In a similar way, what is assessed is open to considerable variation. It may focus on written performances, non-written performances, institutional adjustment or perceived personal character : it may centre on the processes of learning, adapting, thinking or reviewing, or on an end-product such as written right answers. The form of the final assessment may vary from examination certificates, to references, to reports, to whole profiles of skills and achievements, to portfolios of work completed, to self report profiles.

It comes as a shock to find that what seems the inevitable selection of assessment in our own society is absent from other societies. It seems unquestionable that there should be external examinations such as the G.C.S.E. and the G.C.E.'A'level, so to find that another Western European country abandoned this idea over thirty years ago in favour of teacher/pupil/parent compiled profiles, and saved itself a huge quantity of money to spend on actual learning facilities as a result, can be startling.

As in the case of the other dimensions of educational activity, assessment presents us with a wide range of possibilities : a more flexible approach to education would constantly consider and reconsider the appropriateness of each option rather than treat the situation as a board game where the rules and options have all been decided in advance.

The Agenda of Aims.

Since the general aims and more narrowly focused objectives of education have been listed in long taxonomies of which the most substantial, Bloom's Taxonomy of Educational Objectives, fills three volumes, it will come as no surprise that there is little consensus as to the prior aims of education. This can be illustrated in the ideas as to who is fit to teach. The current U.K. requirement is that you are unfit to teach unless you have high grades in G.C.E. 'A' levels, a G.C.E. 'O' level in Maths and in English, and go on to achieve a degree level qualification with a subject identity .(There is no actual evidence that this produces effective teachers and the one longitudinal study of teaching careers that we have by Cortis, rather suggest the reverse.) Robert Owen thought differently and for him the fact that a person was not yet able to read and write too well was not as important as the judgment that they were fit company for children. Other European countries have recently moved away from the notion of a strong subject identity and required teachers to train as general pedagogues with general competence across a range of the subjects as well as capable of facilitating integrated learning on contemporary cross-subject issues such as pollution, the mass media, terrorism, and technology.

A list of educational aims may include some of the following :

1. Preparation for conformity to life in a society as it presently exists.
2. Preparation to perpetuate and spread the current form of society.
3. Preparation to change society through research and innovation.
4. Preparation to be adaptable to changes that occur in an uncertain future.
5. Preparation for the needs of the economy and its manpower planning.
6. Preparation for economic activity as a consumer.
7. Preparation for leisure.
8. Preparation for life as a participating citizen in a democratic society.
 (for democratic we could substitute communist, fascist, capitalist, etc.,)
9. Preparation for personal autonomy and personal development.
10. Preparation for living out a particular religion's prescriptions.

It will come as no surprise to find that schools, educationalists, parents, pupils, employers, politicians, societies and its institutions vary in the priority that they put on these aims as well as any requirement that one or more of them be excluded, for the society for which pupils are to be prepared is seen in terms of rival visions. It may be seen as one of traditional inequality where pupils are to be allocated to the roles of rulers or ruled according to birth or patronage. Again the society may be seen as in a more fluid state of inequality, with mobility for some based on selection often via competition in the education system. Other visions stress equality, or democracy, or a pluralistic tolerating a variety of religious and social creeds. Accordingly, the idea that there is a politically neutral view of education is reserved for the simple minded.

Political compromises can be achieved : although capitalism and democracy are contradictory ideas, the effective compromise achieved in Sweden is that of democratic welfare capitalism where the forces of the free market are deliberately harnessed to serve democratic and welfare requirements. The Quaker business enterprises in the U.K. e.g. Cadbury, Fry and Rowntree, originally worked on similar principles, and some Swedes declare that is where they got the idea in the first place.

Organisation Through Contracts.

The organisation of situations for learning presents a wide ranges of concerns ranging from fundamental issues such as who should make the decisions that are required, to the detail of the decisions themselves e.g. the timetable of activities. The detailed decisions turn out to be legion . How will records of activities and individuals progress be kept? Is new clothing needed, such as uniform? Are there to be rewards or punishments? Will people need to be organised into groups of some kind? How can resources be organised? How will the programme of studies be decided? There are many more, so that manuals of educational decision-making now exist and management courses for teachers are widely available.

Decision-making as regards organisational matters has often been thought to be somewhat simplified by having power and responsibility concentrated in a one or a few hands, the headteacher or the senior staff, and authoritarian structures have been favoured on this and other grounds. In a more flexible approach to education, such an approach may well be seen as only a temporary expedient rather than as the only or the permanent solution. The crucial organisational activity is likely to revolve around the concept of the contract.

Currently, the contract is usually imposed and coercive. If parents decide to send their children to school rather than educate them at home then they more or less have to accept the terms that the school lays down. The legal case histories show that in the U.K. courts regularly favour the decisions of the school staff against the supposed rights or claims of parents or pupils.

An alternative is the negotiated contract. In some educational situations this is already in use . In the case of the Open University, learners are provided with information on courses available, study centres, summer schools, resources , sources of advice and counselling and anything else needed to develop an agreed programme of studies. Ways of revising this initial contract are also made available and regular opportunities for the confirmation or renegotiation of provisional decisions made at an earlier stage are built into the system. All this becomes such a routine and taken-for-granted part of the system that few reflect on the fact that this is contract establishing and a form of negotiating machinery at all.

In contrast, Watts (1980) offers as a basis for a contract, a draft covenant for 'all those in upper secondary schooling' although there is no need to see it as restricted to this age group:

"A Covenant for upper secondary schools whereby it is granted

A. to all students that they

1. will have full access to all the resources for learning both in and out of school , and regardless of which school they attend;
2. will have maximum access to the teachers they may learn from , regardless of whether or not what they want to learn is examinable;
3. will have maximum of choice of whom they wish to work with;
4. will have a choice of what they want to study;
5. will be assured of facilities for work and study free from disruption;
6. will be given every encouragement to develop their own style of work and take responsibility for organising their own patterns of learning and leisure;

7. will have full professional encouragement, instruction, guidance and assessment, not only by formal examination but by assessment of performance over a period of or course;
8. will be free from examinations whose necessity is not demonstrable;
9. will be encouraged in self-assessment;
10. will be respected by teachers for what they are, not for what they will be, or will produce; that they will be regarded as persons not products;
11. will be free to express honest emotions, to discover who they are;
12. will be free from the restrictive labelling of I.Q. or other artificial limiting descriptions of global ability, such as streaming produces;
13. will be free from the threat of corporal punishment or other forms of retribution and humiliation;
14. will be free to dress as they please;
15. will be free to express and argue points of view or political conviction;
16. will be free to assemble and express collective points of view;
17. will be free to comment, critically and constructively, on their teachers;
18. will be encouraged to play an active part in the formulation of the school's aims and the planning of its curriculum, participating with their teachers, and with representation on the governing body;
19. will be protected from political or religious indoctrination;
20. will be enabled to work and live in collaboration with rather than competition with each other;

B to all teachers that they

1. will have the maximum opportunity to participate in the formulation of aims, policy-making, and organisation of the school, thus collectively determining, with their students, the internal conditions of work;
2. may expect that all members of the teaching staff teach;
3. will have means of easy communication with everyone else on the staff;
4. will be given opportunities and encouraged to develop their skills, teaching, social and managerial, within the organisation for the school;
5. will have a right of appeal to their colleagues against decisions taken by anyone else or other groups on staff;
6. may expect students and teachers to show mutual respect for each other;
7. will be allowed time at regular intervals to make collective and unhurried reappraisals of aims and progress;
8. may feel encouraged to send their own children to the school where they teach, free of anxiety or embarrassment;
9. will be given opportunity to exchange visits (a) with teachers in other schools, (b) with people working in other occupations;
10. will have a large say in the selection of fellow teachers and the Head or Principal;

C. to all parents that they

1. will become partners with their sons and daughters, and their teachers in designing the curriculum and in the choices made within it;

2. will be kept regularly informed about the life of the school and the performance of their own children in particular;
3. will be given easy access to the Head and other teachers, with the right to call for ad hoc reports;
4. will have a right to see any other reports relating to them and their children;
5. will be welcome, at reasonable intervals, not just at 'open days', to see the school at normal work;
6. will be informed of career prospects and job openings and to be drawn into consultation at appropriate times;
7. will be able to elect their own representatives on the board of governors, be kept informed by them and have a right of a hearing by the board of governors;
8. will be free from any directive or pressure from school over what their children shall wear, apart from protective clothing where there is a danger to health and safety;
9. will have their children protected at school from interference, assault, humiliation or indoctrination whether by other students, teachers or other users of the school;
10.will be enabled, without restrictive practice, to give the school whatever help the teachers and students would welcome."

When some form of general agreement of this kind is established, the details of the day-to-day programme of learning can be developed within its framework. If the Open University can do it for approaching 100,000 students with the aid of computers, it is surely defeatist to argue that it cannot be done in schools with much smaller populations.

Conclusion

The development of flexibility in the dimensions discussed in this chapter suggest the possibility that the word 'school' is increasingly dated and inadequate to identify an appropriate institution for education in a complex post-industrial society like our own. Perhaps we should begin to see such institutions as *Learning Resource Centres* modelled on the Public Library concept rather that the military regimental model that was adopted in the 1870's when mass schooling was established.

Chapter Seven.

Conclusion - Education For a Changing Future?

"Civilisation is a race between education and catastrophe"

H.G. Wells

At the outset we examined the view that some of the rigidity of the education system stems from its origins in the 1870's when, with considerable plausibility at the time, the authoritarian approach to the organisation of schools was the one that was widely regarded as the right way to go about education. During the last ten years, in some countries, e.g. Canada and Denmark, state systems of education have facilitated a more diverse approach by financing a range of alternative schools, to try to get away from what were increasingly seen as outdated ideas. The Danish Parliament voted in 1987 to spend £38 million on a four year experiment to develop the country's 'school of the future'. In both countries, the probability has been recognised that education is not a problem to which a simple answer can be found, but a complex problem which requires a complex answer.

In the cases of these two countries, ideologies of education are seen as in some state of rivalry so that one school adopts one approach and another an alternative so that they can be compared and choices made. In the famous experiment of this kind in Sweden, one half of Stockholm had one kind of education and the other half another so that a choice could be made after a few years on the basis of the achievements.

The notion of flexischooling contains an attempt to avoid such either /or problems or simplistic solutions. The proposal is that the various authoritarian, democratic and autonomous groups of ideas about education are to some extent, complementary rather than in absolute rivalry and that a flexible approach can allow them all to be on offer, sometimes in a phased arrangement, sometimes as alternatives to provide a choice.

The first idea of a phased arrangement is contained in Russell's ideas about education which were developed in response to what was seen as the rather freewheeling approach of A.S.Neill. Russell argued that education could operate as control in the spirit of freedom in order to move by the acquistion of experience and knowledge into a state of freedom. This latter state of freedom was seen as a state of enlightened freedom rather than the raw freedom that A.S. Neill was thought to favour. Thus Russell saw authoritarian approaches as early phases of education and as temporary expedients, which could service the move towards and the achievement of autonomous and democratic states. His verdict on the existing system would presumably be the same now as then : the temporary expedient of an authoritarian approach had been mistakenly adopted as the final solution.

The second idea of choosing amongst alternatives is currently practised in the private sector of U.K. education, which has many features that are regularly criticised, but in terms of flexischooling, it has a more flexible pattern in offering a variety educational approaches provided in different schools so that parents can choose and pay for the one they deem appropriate. Unlike the Canadian and Danish state systems, no such variety currently exists in the U.K. state provision and the seemingly dated thinking behind the imposition of a National Curriculum does seem to make such a development more difficult.

It may seem odd to argue that visions of education that have been seen as staunch rivals are not necessarily so at all, especially when so much bitter and polarised debate has taken place over this issue in the past, with the 'Black Paper' writers at loggerheads with the 'Progressives' who are in dispute with the 'Deschoolers' etc.,etc. The reason that they can all be seen to have some part to play can be illustrated thus : the complexities of modern life are such that without the experience of behaving with considerable flexibility, people are at risk. In some situations it is necessary to operate with the logistics of authoritarian behaviour patterns, at other times with democratic and at other with autonomous. It follows that an effective education requires some experience of all these groups of approaches and an awareness of when each one in turn might be appropriate. Perhaps modes of travel can illustrate the point. In an passenger aeroplane, the passengers need to behave according to the authoritarian system of behaviour; the alternatives spell disaster. The same individuals, when they take the wheels of their motor cars, need to behave autonomously for the responsibility of driving is now theirs. In small sailing craft, my friends tell me, the crew that cannot behave cooperatively, with teamwork, with interchange of tasks, with some degree of power sharing and with elements of democratic responsibility, is heading for trouble sooner or later. The same might be said of a camping or mountaineering expedition or even a group holiday.

The experience gathered by families who have been educating their children at home has demonstrated how some of these ideas can be effective. Families frequently begin their home-based education by copying school as they have experienced it, with a desk, timetables, and a formal curriculum. Later they have usually become flexible, organising the mornings formally and the afternoons more spontaneously. Even later, many families have learnt to operate across the whole spectrum of curriculum possibilities, selecting the one seen to be appropriate for the particular task in hand. Thus families I have observed have been engaged in learning experiences sometimes in an authoritarian manner, sometimes in a democratic way and at other times adopting autonomous methods. The parents have become flexible in their role, occasionally acting as a teacher instructor, sometimes as a facilitator and other times as a co-learner.

Home-based education has demonstrated other possibilities : families have established written 'contracts' with local educational authority, although they have not been called contracts as such. Members of Education Otherwise are strongly advised to cooperate with the L.E.A. and provide a written statement of their proposed educational approach along with any outline programme they intend. These are then used as the basis of any negotiation as well as subsequent dialogue when officials arrange visits to see the family concerned.

In terms of varied locations for learning, families have been innovative. Finding a time when everyone is at home has proved to be a problem for research purposes because members of the family may be engaged in learning at the local library, the museum, a workplace, with another family in their home, or elsewhere in the community. The whole range of learner roles outlined earlier is also in evidence in the behaviour of many of these families. The flexibility such families develop can lead to situations where they resolve problems that schools frequently find intractable. An example is that of sexism : in contrast to the practice of many schools, families can and do develop equal access to skills whatever the sex of the person concerned. One family had as a project the renovation of the family car which was stripped down to the last nut and bolt and rebuilt, hiring or borrowing equipment for welding or whatever else was needed. The one daughter commented that the only other girl she knew who had learnt to do welding and car mechanics was her sister. She had become aware that none of the local girls she met who went to school had done so.

It would be all to easy to construe all this as another attack on teachers. There are two reasons why I would refute this. One is that teachers are required to work to out of date blueprints . In teacher training these blueprints persist, alternatives not being allowed on the agenda by local and central accreditation committees. They then inevitably form the expected practice of schools. Moreover, the action of politicians in passing legislation confirming such models can hardly be blamed on teachers. In a word, teachers are victims.

The second reason is that some teachers have tried, usually against heavy odds, to develop more flexible approaches. Braving hostile and hysterical journalists, the unimaginative reactions of H.M.I.'s (themselves victims of the system), and incredulous colleagues, they have sought to break out of the existing rigidities.. Thus ideas like Community Education, Parental Involvement Schemes, the Portage Scheme, the educational practice of Special Units for school refusers, the operation of Minischools within schools, are all examples of more flexible educational practice developed not from the home-schooling movement but from within schools. Indeed the answer to those who say flexischooling could never happen, is that substantial elements of it are already here.

A full blown flexischooling might be quite a dazzling sight. It would mean that all the dimensions discussed would be operational with the whole range of possibilities being exploited :

- parents would not be defined as part of the problem, but as part of the solution. The whole range of parental roles in education would be on offer with some operating as para-professional aides, some as partners working to agreed contracts, some as the prime educators in consultation with the school, some as governors if such bodies as governing bodies continue to be seen as of any utility in a more flexible situation.

- the fact that children can learn a great deal without a teacher being present and without teachers would be taken seriously so that the whole range of learner roles would be utilised. Learners would be seen sometimes as partners, at other times as autonomous explorers, sometimes as democratic explorers, occasionally as raw material and as receptacles and rarely if at all as resisters.

- teaching would cease to be defined predominantely as instructing and the whole range of roles that can be seen as facilitating learning would be in use. Teachers, as a body, would be operating a range of authoritarian roles whether consultative, organisational, expert, charismatic or parental, as well as the complex and more professionally demanding non-authoritarian roles as facilitators of autonomous learning or of democratic learning.

- the learning programme would make some use of all the types of curriculum including the imposed subjects, the imposed interpretative, the confidence building, the consultative, the negotiated and the democratic.

- school, as we currently know it, would have been transformed into a learning resources centre using all the repertoire of resources available in the modern world, making use of all possible locations for learning at home and in the community, with the whole range of aims and assessments on offer. The main organisational device would be a negotiated learning contract involving the parents, the teachers and the learners.

It would be foolish to think existing schools could achieve such a range of flexibility overnight although the journey would be shorter for some than others. Schools that have adopted some of the various concepts of community education will already have made a start. One practical use of this book would be to locate the present situation of a school and identify the areas of most extreme rigidity as well as the areas of relative flexibility. . This would enable a particular school to consider which dimension to develop first and which can be left until later.

To those struggling with the day-to-day survival issues like the shortage of materials, implementing severely outdated governmental ideas about education, coping with truancy, meeting the pressures of new examination procedures, tolerating a number of time-serving and cynical colleagues, coping with journalists on national newspapers with plenty of destructive power but little sense of responsibility, the issue of transforming education may seem rather exotic. The rate of change in modern society suggests it is not. As an indication consider that in the early 1970's the idea of an Open University was held by a few imaginative people and it was widely ridiculed. Yet it has now become the largest university in the U.K. by far - over five times bigger that any other.

Sadly, in the process it seems to have lost a lot of its innovative drive and perhaps could do with becoming more flexible itself.

There are many scenarios envisaged for the future of the U.K., some optimistic some pessimistic. They include :

- regression to some previous state now interpreted as a golden age

- perpetuation of the status quo with little social change

- gradual economic decline as the last major natural resource of oil goes

- moves towards a self sufficiency economy as scarce resources dwindle

- as a result of the micro-processor revolution, less work and more leisure and the need for more population control through a police state

- the micro-processor revolution being resolved by developing responsible autonomy and a more even access to resources, as an alternative to a police state

- nuclear holocaust either by accident or by intent leading to a society of small groups of self sufficient tribes with a short life expectancy.

A regressive education system increases the possibility of one of the pessimistic outcomes happening and it can be identified by the kind of people produced described graphically by Postman and Weingartner (1969) in these terms :

" the students who endure it come out as passive, acquiescent, dogmatic, intolerant, authoritarian, inflexible, conservative personalities who desperately need to resist change in a effort to keep their illusion of certainty intact."

A more flexible education system increases the possibility of one of the more optimistic outcomes happening since the people produced are more likely to exhibit the active, inquiring, flexible, adaptable, free-thinking, imaginative and innovative characteristics that these require.

Can we afford the risks of an education system that stares intently into the past as the world rockets into the future ? Could flexischooling be the only intelligent option open ? Or, taking up the proposition of H.G.Wells, do we prefer disaster to education ?

FLEXISCHOOLING IN PRACTICE

THE THEORY OF FLEXISCHOOLING which Roland Meighan has laid out requires working models of practice. Dame Catherine's School in Ticknall in South Derbyshire may be offered as a model which could be adapted to suit practically any social circumstance.

We opened on Sep 8th 1987 with 12 students from 41/2 to 16 years old. Now, a year later, we have grown to 35 students. We are nearly at our limit of numbers. We wish to remain small in order to retain that closeness of relationship which we believe underpins all human personal development in an educational sense.

We do, however, wish to put out small satellite learning groups which accept our principles, to work in association with us. We aim to grow without expansion. We would like some of these satellite groups in their turn to become small schools like our own, and to put out their own satellites. We are trying to found an "Education Now" Development and Support Centre to initiate, develop and support this process.

The advantage of this method of growth is that it will enable a network of small learning groups to cover the country within a few years. We want to work alongside the maintained system as a complementary part of it rather than as an alternative sector of education. We do not thnk that what we are doing is in any way extraordinary or special. We think it derives from simple common-sense and from self-evident assertions about the nature of human beings and the way we learn and are nurtured in family groups within the community we thereby begin to create.

The "Education Now" Development and Support Centre(s) will therefore be available to the Maintained sector schools as well. Teachers will be able to join the independent cooperatives which will run them.."teachers" in the sense that they are skilled, or are becoming skilled in the facilitation of learning, rather than just those who have been trained to pass on to others a body of knowledge, according to a banking theory of learning.

Support will be offered to the "Micro-School", such as Dame Catherine's in Ticknall. It will also be offered, even more crucially, to the small Satellite Learning Groups being operated by parents and teachers, or by parents who are teachers in their own homes, or in rooms of buildings which are being used as the base for such tiny schools. See Diag. 1.

These ideas for the future development of a whole complementary system of education are not the fanciful contrivance of heady youth. The idea is that many small schools, many minute satellite learning groups and all sorts of independent education development centres should interact to enable a lived experience of education to permeate society. These are logical developments from the demand that parents are making to have their children at Dame Catherine's School. We have been bombarded with requests by parents wishing to move house to have their children

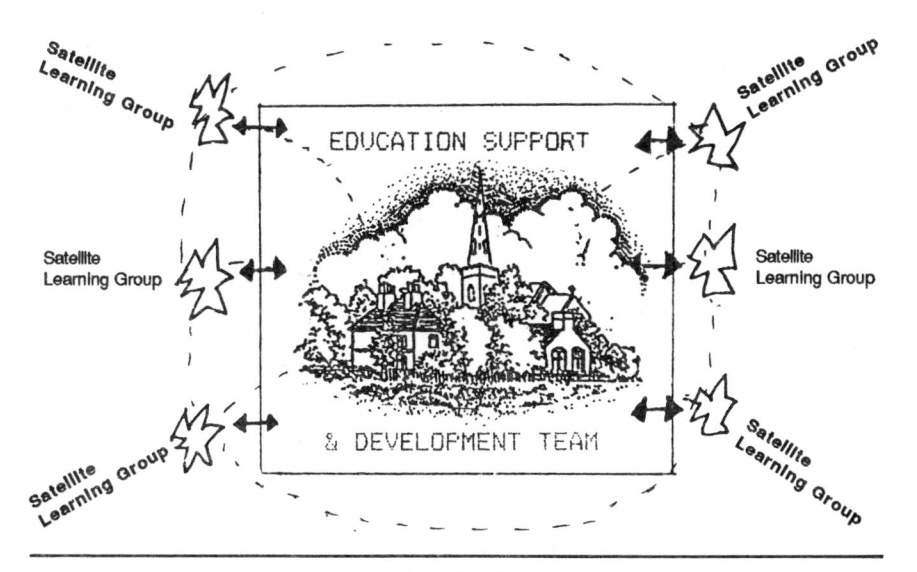

DIAGRAM 1.

educated in the way Roland Meighan has been describing. Parents have begged to be allowed to pay and have been bitterly disappointed when we have had to say that we exist for children of our locality and that there are limits to our expansion even for them.

There are of course, limits to the number of experimental small schools that can be funded by Trusts to provide models for others to follow. Sooner or later, the state will have to consider giving a reality to the rhetoric of parental choice so that small schools provided by parents may be funded by the public purse as in Denmark where 85% of the running cost of such schools is paid by the state. Eventually the idea that the state should provide all education except private education will have to go. What is needed is for the state to support a diverse range of educational provision so that parental involvement can take place and actual provision can be from a variety of different agencies. This would suit our emerging pluralistic society and the pace of economic and technological change.

To date there are several different sorts of educational ventures which are depending on Charitable funding to try to establish these principles of practice without the snare of being private schools.

There is the Small School in Hartland, Devon, now entering its seventh year. Hartland is a small school for children from 11 to 16 years old. There is the small school at Abinger Hammer, in Sussex, for children from 3 to 8 years old. A small school is opening this September in the centre of Liverpool for secondary children. In remote Scorag, in Western Scotland, the Local Education Authority has given in to the pleas of the local parents to be able to found their own small local school instead of having to send their children to distant boarding schools. This is the only example of the Local Authority funding such a school. Funding was given on the basis of travel costs saved...not because of any clear appreciation that in any case it was likely that such a school was intrinsically better. There are of course the many Steiner Waldorf schools to which parents contribute an agreed percentage of their income annually.

Dame Catherine's is a relatively new comer on the scene. It is one year old. It has several unique features:

- ○ that it is the only one of the new "human scale" schools to be for all ages. We take children from 4½ to 16 years.

- ○ that it is also the only one which has a clear intention to replicate and to work out a way of doing this (by Satellite Learning Centres, Microschools and Education Development and Support centres).

- ○ that the parents are founding a retail business in which their voluntary cooperative labour will help fund the school.

- ○ that the school will become "buddy schools" with the City-As-School in New York and will exchange students for work experience modules of seven weeks duration from the New Year 1989 if the necessary travel sponsorship is forthcomimg.

- ○ that the parents will develop a group exchange programme with 15 parents and their children in Burgundy, France, doing "Education Sans Ecole" including children from 8 years old upwards.

- ○ that it is the only one to open a parent managed Learning Club for adults on its premises.

- ○ that the educational principles behind Flexischooling, Minischooling in big schools and Smallschooling are expounded and published in a national magazine edited by the Head of Dame Catherine's in a cooperative publishing venture "Education Now".

All this has happened in the last 12 months, the first year of Dame Catherine's existence.

When Annabel, my wife, and I, were invited by a few of the parents of the 9 children in the doomed Ticknall Primary School to re-open the school as an independent, all-ages, school operating under the ancient Trust provisions of the 1744 benefactress, Dame Catherine Harpur Crewe, (that the school should "provide for the free education of the young people of Ticknall and Calke and the surrounding parishes"), we had spent two years working at the Small School in Hartland. I had been invited by the Schumacher Society to coordinate a movement to be known as the Human Scale Education movement in 1985. My two years as coordinator had culminated in a National Conference at the Oxford Poly which took place for 3 days just before we opened the school in Ticknall.

The three main planks of the movement were:

☐ Small schools (both the preservation of those in existence but under threat and the foundation of new ones by the Danish system of financing).

☐ Minischools (to make human scale structures possible in very large schools so that they became federations of minischools on one site).

☐ Flexischooling (to link the human scale structures of the large institutions with the small schools and with other processes of education within the community).

Our tricolour flag would have celebrated "Smallschooling, Minischooling and Flexischooling". We were above all concerned that the movement should have relevance to the whole system of education. We wished to appeal to both the "Education Otherwise" wing and to the people and parents whose children were in the giant size state schools (one should say "locally maintained schools" but perhaps more appropriately "locally supported and centrally starved schools" would be nearer the mark!).

We had little time to prepare for the opening of Dame Catherine's School. What little time we had was spent with solicitors fighting off the attempt of the Church of England to sell the building under the misapprehension that the building was Church property. We also travelled to see the Charity Commissioners in Liverpool with our solicitor to set on foot a managing Trust to do the day to day work for the 1744 Trust. We had 1½ days in London buying a Maths and Reading course, ½ a day engaging another teacher to help us get started and a day meeting parents and clearing out the Local Education Authority's relics.

We started with 12 children, of whom 5 were in Education Otherwise as the responsibility of their parents. These 5 attended part-time and are not on our register. We had no certain financing, merely some rather fanciful assurances of support, most of which were unfulfilled.

We have now survived a year, have 35 children, of whom 5 are "Flexi" and we have an almost daily barrage of telephone calls from parents who are eager to get their children's names down. Of the 35 children, 2 have "special needs" in that if they were not with us they would each be requiring full time assistance from one skilled adult. Because they are in our atmosphere of an extended family these two are making astonishing progress and are not only fully accepted by the other children but are contributing to the school a great deal by their presence even if they do take up more of the attention of adults than anyone else.

It is not possible to separate the material aspects of the school from the social and individual benefits that accrue in a daily practice of education in this frame. The very urgency of the need that we have in the school for all sorts of things that will not be there unless they are directly provided by the parents or local people generates the community discipline and high morale that is evident at every moment of the day when we are working together with the parents in the school.

Community as the sharing of a common predicament is there all the time. This togetherness pervades not only the time we spend in school but spreads between the children in the village after school, between the parents socially and between us as teachers and the parents and local people, a growing number of whom are beginning to support what we are about.

This is not a product of theory; it is a product of experience: we did what we had to do to start working as a school and the daily work welds us together into a community. In this, the effect on the young parents in their emerging perception of the possibilities in the education of their children, is one of the main and least expected outcomes of what we are doing.

I remember as a boy in the Second World War, during the Bristol Blitz, feeling the same sense of the unity of purpose in adversity as we emerged from yet another night huddled together under the dining room table as the bombs showered down. Less dramatically, perhaps, I remember the feeling of common purpose at Madeley Court, in the most depressed area of Telford New Town, how the parents used to work in the minischool reorganised school and raised #30,000 annually audited through school funds towards their own small minischools. Similarly I remember in the Navy during National Service, how the atmosphere and informal operational discipline was so evident on submarines or in the diving section, and was so absent on the vast, non-operational shore establishments.

Small scale is no panacea; it prevents less than large scale: properly managed it yields the circumstances for real social cooperation and for the realisation of individual identity. It provides the conditions for the transformation of alienation into engagement: the opposite of Sartre's "L'enfer...c'est les autres". After one year of work at Dame Catherine's I write with profound gratitude that what so many become teachers for (and so rarely experience) it has been our privilege to experience this year....that real active partnership between students, parents, teachers and local people which leads to learning.

This, then above all has been the lesson of the year at Dame Catherine's; that this way lies genuine participation by parents. An unexpected, but very welcome spin-off has been the evidence of very fast and well rooted progress in all the basics of reading, writing, Maths, Science and so on. It leads one to suppose that perhaps the real single most to be desired educational reform in the state would be the doubling of the numbers of teachers in the classroom. But I do not think that this alone would effect the required transformation. We do have a very good pupil-teacher ratio, but it is the full participation by parents, by the 18 local people who regularly come in to give us a hand, and by the older children in the learning of the younger ones which really effects the phenomenal progress that we have seen.

The mixed age aspect of the school is very important. The older children read daily with the younger ones after lunch for a ½ hour. They become skilled communicators with the very young. They have carried out a story writing project with them, listening to their ideas for a story and then going away to work it up, write it out and read it back. They help with games, with fun on the playground, with interaction at the twice weekly whole school meetings. They joke and cuddle and help with cut fingers and knees.

Mixed age learning gives the lie to the age group living which we engage in today. It restores human proportion, variety of response and of emotion to the daily round. The older children help with building and decoration jobs in the group room of the younger groups...they do the advanced technical bits on the models for the youngest group...they cook...they clean...they "look out" for the little ones. There is not only the mixed age aspect among the children, but amongst the adults too. So many and varied ages help in the school! And people who are not at all like teachers!

All the cleaning, playground supervision, maintenance and repairs are done by the parents on a signing up rota basis. Whole families come in to clean, grannies, grandads, aunts and the toddlers. Many a crucial comment is passed as the pan is held by the teacher for the brush to sweep into. We can surely say that the channel of communication now goes on within the parent body and has no need to depend on the teacher as a clearing house for action.

For the younger ones the parents are kept fully in the picture, are consulted and participate at least twice a day in the curriculum discussions and comments on progress. The first quarter of an hour of the school day is a buzz not at the school gate but right in the school itself. This is repeated at the end of school. It is often carried on throughout the sessions of craft, woodwork, pottery, music, drama, reading, writing or whatever, since the parents also work in the room from time to time as well.

It might be said that the village school lacks the advanced facilities to do science properly with the secondary age range. I suspect that there are benefits to science learning from this absence of expensive equipment.

I recall one week where the subject was electricity and after a 1½ hour discussion with a local doctor of science present, the following day her husband (a keen astronomer) brought in a small electric motor, carefully made from 2 paper clips, a battery, a magnet and a small amount of copper wire. This was eagerly discussed and the theory of its working ivestigated in science encylopaedias.

The problem was then posed that they should do a presentation on the following day to the middle (Primary age range group) and get small groups to construct their own motors. They prepared their visual aids, equipment and motor kits like enthusiastic beginner teachers and each took turns to explain different parts. At the end they had delivered an interesting session and had been forced to come to grips with the fundamentals of electricity. They were ready to do more advanced work on a programmed Open Learning course.

We share the key experiences across the age range. If my older (secondary age group) goes away on a camping expedition, or spends a week making a video film,the outcomes are reported, or the film shown at a whole school meeting. If two of my group go away to Lugano as the UK reps on the first international children's Peace Council, this is the opportunity for the whole school to construct a booklet on peace and to bind it together.

The opportunity for education in the local environment is obviously much greater in such a small group environment with parents at hand to help where possible. Similarly working in the local community is very possible. Community service becomes a reality, as with the older group's Village magazine "Our Ticknall" which is now awaited with curiosity and mounting interest.Respect for the environment ,for each other and for the local people.............

All this and so much more is possible. We have open access and are non-selective. Within the school we are three small schools which interact and merge as necessary. Using evening classes, distance learning National Extension College courses and Open Learning techniques we can cover a fair range of GCSE'S.....as many as a normal comprehensive school.

Last Friday term ended. We reconstructed the classroom of the Primary group while they and the infants went on an outing. In the evening we went ice skating in the Nottingham Ice Stadium. Yesterday a group of parents did a sponsored parachute jump. Next Wednesday we are holding a meeting to discuss the imminent opening of the shop the parents are starting.......and so it goes on....a happy and hard working community of education.

The practice of the Flexischooling of which Roland Meighan has written!

References

Blishen, E. (1969) *The School That I'd Like*. Harmondsworth : Penguin

Boulter, H. (1984) 'Parents and children : 100 Years of the parents' National Education Union and its World-wide Education Service' in Harber,C., Meighan,R. and Roberts,B. (1984) *Alternative Educational Futures*. London : Holt,Rinehart and Winston.

Cortis,G. (1977) *The Social Context of Teaching*. London : Open Books.

Freire,P. (1972) *Pedagogy of the Oppressed*. Harmondsworth : Penguin.

Goodman,P. (1971) *Compulsory Miseducation*. Harmondsworth : Penguin.

Handy,C. (1984) *Taken for Granted? Understanding Schools as Organisations*.
York : Longmans.

Hemming,J. (1980) *The Betrayal of Youth*. London : Marion Boyers.

Hemming,J. (1984) 'The Confidence-building Curriculum' in Harber,C.,Meighan,R.and Roberts,B. (1984) *Alternative Educational Futures*.
London : Holt, Rinehart and Winston.

Hillery,C. (1955) 'Definitions of community' *Rural Sociology* 20.

Holt,J. (1982) *Teach Your Own*. Brightlingsea : Lighthouse Books.

Husen,T.(1979) *The School in Question*. Oxford : Oxford University Press.

Husen,T. (1985) *The Learning Society Revisited*. Oxford : Pergamon.

Makins,V. (1984) 'Giving the customers a say' *Times Educational Supplement*,
23 November.

Neill,A.S. (1968) *Summerhill*. Harmondsworth : Penguin.

North,R. (1982) 'All the world's a school' *Times Educational Supplement*,9 April

North,R. (1987) *Schools of Tomorrow*. Hartland : Green Books.

Postman,N. and Weingartner,C. (1971) *Teaching as a Subversive Activity*.
Harmondsworth : Penguin.

Rogers,C. (1983) *Freedom to Learn for the '80s*. Columbus,Ohio : Merrill.

Rowland,S. (1984) *The Enquiring Classroom*. Lewes : Falmer.

Rowland,S. (1988) 'Teaching for Learning' *Education Now* 1, pp 18-9

Russell,B. (1916) *Principles of Social Reconstruction*. London : Unwin.

Russell,B. (1926) *On Education*. London : Unwin.

Sharp,R. and Green,A. (1975) *Education and Social Control*. London : Routledge and Kegan Paul

Stone,J. and Taylor,F. (1976) 'The sad tale of pupils' rights' *Where?* 122.

Taylor,L.C. (1971) *Resources for Learning*. Harmondsworth : Penguin.

Toogood,P. (1984) *The Head's Tale*. Telford : Dialogue Publications.

Waterland, L. (1985) *Read With Me*. Stroud : Thimble Press.

Watts,J. (1980) *Towards an Open School*. London : Longman.

Wells,G. and Nicholls,J. (1985) *Language and Learning ; An Interactional Perspective*. Lewes : Falmer.

White,R. and Brockington,D. (1983) *Tales Out of School*. London : Routledge and Kegan Paul.

Widlake,P. and Macleod,F. (1984) *Raising Standards*. Coventry : Community Education Development Centre.

Index

Ability, 5
Aims
  - agenda of, 44-5
  - theories of, 9
Ancestor worship, 34
Assessment
  - theories of, 8, 43-4
Authoritarian education, 27-9, 31, 36, 46, 49, 50
Autonomous education, 5, 9, 19, 23, 25, 29, 49, 50

Belfield Reading Project, 14
Blueprints, dated, 51
Bruner, Jerome, 32

Canada, 49, 50
Capitalism, 9, 45
  - market, 45
  - welfare, 34, 45
Childhood, 20
Child
  - centred, 22, 34
  - referenced, 22, 34
City as School, 8, 37, 41, 43
Community Education, 3-7, 43, 51, 52
Community Development Project, 3, 12
Competition, 6, 9
Computers, 1, 3, 6, 18, 34, 40
Contracts, educational, 2, 15, 25, 40, 45-8, 50, 52

Co-operation, 22
Coventry, 3
Correspondence Colleges, 2, 3, 42
Cultural inertia, 11
Curriculum, 32-9, 52
  - confidence building, 35-6
  - consultative, 36-7
  - democratic, 38
  - hidden, 16, 24, 32, 34
  - interpretative, 34-5
  - National, 33, 35, 50
  - negotiated, 3, 22, 37-8
  - religious, 9, 33, 45
  - spontaneous, 38
  - subjects, 33, 34

Democracy, 8, 9, 21, 45
Democratic curriculum, 24-5, 38
Democratic education, 49, 50
Democratic learning, 24-5, 29
    - independent learning co-operative, 24, 30
    - learning co-operative, 24, 30
    - project approach, 24, 30
    - syndicate approach, 24, 30
Denmark, 49, 50
Department of Education and Science (DES), 14, 37
Descartes, 4
Deschooling, 5, 43, 50

Early Childhood Education, 4, 6, 20, 24, 31, 34
Education Act 1944, 1
Education Otherwise, 1, 3, 5, 8, 16, 42, 50
Examinations, 8, 21, 28, 39, 44

Fascism, 34
Flexistudy schemes, 39
Fox Hill Reading Workshop, 14
Fraser, James, 18
Further Education Colleges, 39

(GWS.. , 16)
Govenors, school, 12
Growing Without Schooling (GWS), 2, 16

Haringey Reading Project, 14
Hemming, James, 4, 31, 35

Hidden curriculum, 16, 24, 32, 34
Holt, John, 2, 16, 17, 19
Homes, 3, 4
Home-based education (see also Education Otherwise), 1, 2, 3, 5, 14, 15, 22, 24, 39, 40, 50
Home teaching service, 3
Homework, 4
Husen, Torsten, 5, 20

Ideologies of Education, 5-9, 49
Impression management, 13
Individualised learning, 4
Inequality, 9, 23, 45
Innovations, 3

Knowledge
- explosion, 18
- theories of, 5-6, 35

Learners
- as autonomous explorers, 19, 23
- as client, 19, 21
- as democratic explorers, 19, 24, 25
- as partners, 19, 22
- as raw material, 19, 21
- as receptacles, 19, 20
- as resisters, 19
- consultation with, 22
- rights of, 21
- viewpoint of, 22

Learning
- active, 34
- apprenticeship approach, 15
- autonomous, 23-4, 29-30
- co-operative, 6, 22
- democratic, 24 -5, 38
- dialogue, 25, 34
- individualised, 23-4, 29-30
- as research 23, 24, 38
- Resource Centres, 40-8, 52
- self-directed 23-4, 29-30
- theories of, 6, 18-26, 52

Local Education Authorities, 3, 39, 50
Location 2, 3, 7, 17, 40, 42-3, 51
Locke, 4, 20

Management, 46
Manpower Services Commission, 3, 38
Mason, Charlotte, 14, 40, 42
Mass Media, 4, 6, 11, 18, 34, 40
Mass Schooling, 4, 11, 40, 42, 48
Mead, Margaret, 16
Menuhin, Yehudi, 16
Minischools, 51
Monopoly, game of, 43

Northampton L.E.A., 37
Neill, A.S., 49

Open University, 3, 8, 24, 28, 42, 46, 48, 52
Organisation, 8
Owen, Robert, 44

Parkway Programme, 7, 41, 43
Parent sector
- as para-professional aide , 12
- as partner, 2, 12, 13, 14
- as pre-school educator, 12, 15
- as prime educator, 12, 16
- as police, 12
- as problem, 2, 12
Parents, 1, 2, 3, 4, 6, 11-17, 46, 50, 51-2
- National Education Union (PNEU), 14, 40
- theories of, 7, 11-17
- the "good", 12
Partnership, 2
Part-time schooling, 1, 2
Politicians, 51
Portage scheme, 51
Power sharing, 29
Primary school, 23
Private sector, 50
Profiles, 8, 44

Psychology, 4
Public Library model, 48
Punishment, 6
Pupils, see learners
    - unions, 37

Quakers, 45

Radio, 3, 7, 11, 18, 40, 42
Religion, 9, 33, 45
Regressive education, 53
Resources, 3, 4, 40-8
    - theories of, 7
Resources Centres, 40-8, 52
Rigidity and schooling, 2, 5, 9, 10, 49
Russell, Bertrand, 33, 34, 49

Secondary school, 23
Sexism, 51
Schools Council General Studies Project, 4
Schools
    - models of, 4
Simulations, 4
Society
    - pluralistic, 9
Sweden, 9, 34, 37, 41, 45, 49

Teacher
    - authoritarian, 27-9, 31, 36
    - autocratic, 27
    - charismatic, 28
    - consultative, 28
    - democratic, 29
    - expert, 28
    - non-authoritarian, 29-30
    - organisational, 28
    - parental, 27-8
Teachers, 6, 11, 15
    - roles of, 6, 27-31, 52
    - as victims, 51
Teaching
    - as facilitation, 3
    - as instruction, 3, 4, 18
    - as learning consultant, 6
    - theories of, 6
Television, 3, 4, 7, 11, 18, 35, 40, 42
Textbooks, 5
Timetables, 6, 8, 37
Technical and Vocational Educational Initiative (TVEI), 3

U.S.A., 2, 7, 16, 17, 22, 24, 41, 43
U.S.S.R., 34
University, Open, 3, 8, 24, 28, 42, 46, 48, 52
University of the Third Age, 30

Wells, H.G., 49, 53
Wesley, John, 20, 36
Work, workplaces, 3, 18
Work experience, 41, 42
World-wide Education Service (WES), 2, 3, 14, 15, 16, 40

Youth Training Scheme (YTS), 3, 38

For publication in Spring 1989...

Educational Management and the practice of democracy

Readers of Roland Meighan's FLEXISCHOOLING will be interested in the above-mentioned book to be published in Spring 1988. The book, edited by Clive Harber and Roland Meighan, presents papers by nearly a score of educationists who took part in a symposium on Democratic Practice in Education at Birmingham University in April 1988.

To quote from the Editors' Preface;

"In *authoritarian* education in its various forms, one person (or a small group of persons) makes and implements the decisions about what to learn, when to learn, how to learn, how to assess learning, and the nature of the learning environment.

"In *democratic* education, the learners as a group have the power to make some, most, or even all of these decisions since power is shared and not appropriated in advance by a minority. Ironically, in many countries (including our own) that sustain the illusion that they are very democratic, such educational practices are rare and, indeed, meet with irrational opposition."

In their contributions to this book, those espousing a democratic practice in education do not see it in an unreal way as an ideal state but, paraphrasing Winston Churchill's words, the worst system of organisation and order available - *except for all the alternatives*. Drawbacks, such as the consumption of a considerable time in debate, dialogue and decision making, are admitted but the conclusion is that democratic practice is certainly the lesser of evils. It is an approach which is sorely needed if education is to to be regenerated in a way appropriate to the times we live in.

(Further details from Education Now, P.O. Box 186, Ticknall, Derbyshire DE7 1WF)

EDUCATION NOW

EDUCATION NOW is a bi-monthly magazine issued to subscribers.

The editorial team believes that parents, teachers and all those concerned with education need to be refreshed by reading about the more hopeful side of educational developments. There has been much concentration on the disturbing difficulties being experienced in the present scene but very real, constructive opportunities exist.

EDUCATION NOW reports on positive initiatives which are occurring here and abroad. It provides a platform for fresh ideas and actively promotes a dialogue in education by inviting contributions by readers.

The Editor is Philip Toogood, former Editor of "Dialogue in Education", author of "The Head's Tale", winner of the Institute of Social Invention 1st Prize (Education Section) for Minischools, Founding Chairman of the Community Education Association, first Coordinator of the Human Scale Education movement and widely experinced as a teacher and activator in varied educational fields - including Warden of Swavesey Village College in Cambridgeshire, Head of Madeley Court Comprehensive in Telford and current Head of Dame Catherine's School and Education Centre in Derbyshire.

Subscription details from Education Now, P.O.Box 186, FREEPOST, Derby DE7 1XZ (No stamp required).